GOD

IS

Experiencing

YOUR

LIFE

TR GARDONE

GOD IS *Experiencing* YOUR LIFE
By TR Gardone

ISBN: 979-8-218-13861-5

All Rights Reserved. No part of this publication may be reproduced or transmitted in any form or by any means without written permission of the author. The author guarantees all contents are original and do not infringe upon the legal rights of any other person or work.

This book is a revision of the original book "Does God (Really) Understand What I'm Going Through" produced in 2015, as originally edited by Jen Meadows. This revision as "God Is Experiencing Your Life" by TR Gardone was edited by Susan McCollum.

Prepared for Publication By

PUBLISHING

MAKING YOUR BOOK A REALITY
Ceder Point, NC | 843-929-8768 | info@BandBpublishingLLC.com

Scripture was taken from The Holy Bible, predominately being the New International Version Translation Copyright 1973, 1978, 1984, 2011 by the International Bible Society, Colorado Springs, Colorado. Used by permission; all rights reserved.

To contact the Author
TR Gardone
Facebook: BIAS-Because It's All Spiritual
Email: BIAS.TRGardone@gmail.com

Contents

ACKNOWLEDGMENTS 1
Thank you

INTRODUCTION 3
Omni-Experience

CHAPTER 1 5
Does God Really Understand What I'm Going Through?
> Been There, Done That - Shared Experiences - Bonding - Together In Adversity - The Identity Of Us (We) - No One Understands What I'm Going Through! - Turn To God? - Including God In "We" - The Identity Of "Us" - Can We Relate To God Or Him To Us? - Like Him, Like Us

CHAPTER 2 31
Does God Really Understand The Loss Of A Loved One?
> The Value of a Relationship - A Valued Relationship - Losing A Loved One - Watching It Happen - The "If's And If Only's" - Why, God? - Why Am I Asking God Why? - The First Question - The Second Question - The Third Question - Moral Credibility - Faithfulness - Touch Me From Your Experience

CHAPTER 3 63
Does God Really Understand My Death?
> Knowing My Dying - The Dying Along The Way - Living In My Dying - Praying In My Dying - Being Truthful In My Dying - Being Faithful In My Dying - Making Provision In My Dying - The Hope and Faith In My Dying - Forgiving In My Dying - The Trust In My Dying - I Haven't Experienced This Before - How To Live In My Dying

CHAPTER 4 85
Does God Really Understand My Temptation And Inner Conflict?
> God Suffered - The Pain Of Resistance - Being Tempted By

Need - The #1 American Temptation - What Can I Get Away With? - My Divided Self - Being Faced With The "No" - An Example Of The Pain Of Resistance - Truthful Confession - Spiritual Points Made

CHAPTER 5 .... **107**
Does God Really Understand Life's Odds 'N' Ends?

Based On A True Story - Socializing And Dialoguing - Confrontation - Paying Taxes - Office And Workplace Politics - Growing A Workforce Ministry - Humanity and Limitations - Traveling - Homelessness - Funding Sources - Being Normal - Family Life - Adultery

CHAPTER 6 .... **129**
Does God Really Understand My Emotions?

Is Anger A Sin? - Jesus Got Angry - Frustration - Frustration And Disappointment - Regrets, Grief, And Heartache - Multiple Emotions - Sorrow - Pushed To Tears

CHAPTER 7 .... **151**
Celebrity

The Greatest Celebrity Who Ever Lived And Still Does, Is Jesus Christ - The Principle That Celebrity Is Built Upon - The Key To Sanity - The Prime Pattern - No Time To Eat - Honest Inventory - Who Is In The Crowd? - (Dis)Connection

CHAPTER 8 .... **173**
The BIRD: Betrayal, Injustice, Rejection, Desertion

Who Is In What Together? - Betrayal - Injustice - Rejection - When Can Rejection Be A Good Thing? - When Rejection Isn't a Good Thing - Desertion - What To Do When You Get The BIRD

CHAPTER 9 .... **193**
The Omni-Experience Of God

He Knows "The Why" - Experiencing Our Lives - The Risk Of Exposure - Creating Distance - Private Property Rights - He's Still There Doing That - God Experiences My Life - His Omni-Experience

SUMMARY **213**

Acknowledgments

Thank you

I have taught the Omni-Experience of God a multitude of times which helped me intuitively, creatively, and combined with my education and life's experience, bring forth this work. I would like to thank Jen Meadows, the professional proofreader of the original 2015 book "Does God (Really) Understand What I'm Going Through?" I would also like to thank the following for this 2023 Revision - - Susan McCollum, editing, and B&B Publishing. Finally, I would like to thank all the mentors, pastors, friends, and my wife who have helped shape my ministry.

Introduction

Omni-Experience

I'm not going to say everything there is to say about God having experienced everything we have, either in practice or principle. I simply wanted to prove through scriptural evidence that God, who came in the form and person of Jesus Christ, has the capacity to experience life as a human adding to the relationship bond he has with us.

This is an encouraging work for those who struggle spiritually with life's issues. I wrote this work to remind us that we are not alone. Our God isn't just observing, he's also participating...not just with us, but in us.

Intro Omni-experience. The Omni-Experience of God is the Doctrine that God experiences everything that we do as he lives in us. To my knowledge, I am the only person, at this point, who teaches this doctrine.

Chapter 1

Does God Really Understand What I'm Going Through?

Each human being experiences events, situations, and circumstances that are considered rough, tough, and even painful to endure. At those times, we may ask "Who are the people, or who is the person, who stands by me? No one wants to go through their valley or trying times in isolation. Individuals can expend only so much spiritual, emotional, mental, and even physical energy on their own before finding themselves exhausted. Spent. Empty. The primary cause is a sense of hopelessness rooted in the reality or the belief (however true or not) that they have no support structure. Alone. Even couples can experience this. What people primarily want is to have the sense that they are not struggling by themselves. Who is in this with me? Couples would answer "We're in this alone." How paradoxical! Even two people may consider themselves "alone." Of course, much of the population would have to admit that they do have others in their lives who give attention to their situation. But those people who give attention to your circumstance may have their efforts and care invalidated or minimized by the outlook or perspective that is internal to the thought-life of the one who is going through something. Why? Some obvious thoughts are that the concern shown is false. Another thought may be that "others may care, but there's nothing they can do that will alleviate or remove my plight." The one that seems to be the front-runner in minimizing or invalidating another's concern is that "they may feel sympathy, compassion, or even pity, but they don't have empathy." Empathy is defined as identification with, and an understanding of, another's situation, feelings, and motives.

Been There, Done That

While people still want sympathy, compassion, and sometimes even pity, what really seems to make the difference are the characteristics of care and concern that are embodied with empathy. We have an intuitive outlook that someone who has experienced what we have gone through, or are going through, usually has an understanding about our predicament that supersedes others' experience. Empathy trumps compassion, sympathy, etcetera. There is something unique about the claim of "been there, done that, bought the T-shirt!" A bond is forged among those of common experiences. Need proof? Just listen to a group of women talking about their war stories of childbirth. "My labor was so bad!" How about hunting stories common among outdoorsmen or the fish that got away? Video players tell stories of video game conquests. There are always the nostalgic references to music, dance, politics, dress, and such, for people who relate to each other in a certain age group or in referring to a certain era. All demographics share internal conversations and share identity factors about themselves as a group.

Shared Experiences

Women share women experiences. Men share men experiences. Married folk share married experiences. Parents share parenting. Workers in a particular field relate to their work culture and environment. Career professionals with similar goals would more than likely develop an affinity toward one another for their career path's fellow travelers and like-minded pursuers. Certain ethnic and economic-class neighborhoods naturally find their history and class structure more familiar. Hispanics to Hispanics. Jews to Jews. African American to African American. Blue collar to blue collar. Every demographic can be broken into sub-groupings. Young marrieds relate more with young marrieds, rather than older marrieds. Soccer players find affinity with each other more than with power lifters. Boating enthusiasts find common bonds more with each other than mountain climbers. The politically interested seek out the politically interested. The subgroups keep subdividing until they find the most common denominators. That's how marriages are formed, partnerships agreed upon, and church denominations founded.

Shared experiences and common interests are identity factors and can also be bonding influences. What we go through shapes our identity and molds our character. Surgeries, unemployment, car wreck, passed up for the job or promotion, in-law problems. What we like to do-- watch movies, eat out, play sports, go to church. What we went through, what we like, or what we like to do together. If we had the same type of medical issue and had the same surgery. If we went to the same college. In a casual conversation with a stranger, you find out the person is from the same community you grew up in or have a strong attraction to, and identity with, perhaps because you lived there for a season of your life. Having common reference points leads us inevitably to some degree of believing we have something in common. Take this example, a young Asian American woman who grew up in an Asian American neighborhood, went to college, has a degree in accounting, has been married to a career engineer for five years, has two children, likes to do scrapbooks and lives in an upscale neighborhood, may find little in common with a high-school educated, middle-aged, blue-collar, union carpenter who has always been single, has no children and likes to hunt and fish. That would seem naturally true on the surface and most people see the disparity. However, what if they both were recovering alcoholics in the same support group? What if he is engaged to her aunt and getting married in three months and will become part of her family? What if they attend the same church and the carpenter and the woman's husband are prayer and accountability partners? Maybe they don't live in the same neighborhood, but they live in the same larger community, share similar political views, or even supported the same candidate for community office. When we examine this further, what at first appears to have a large amount of dissimilarity, now has a great deal of commonality. The differences in experiences, education, work, and obvious ethnic and class variations are outweighed by other shared experiences (alcoholism), viewpoints (politics), beliefs (church), and relationships (her husband and the aunt). While it's legitimate to say the carpenter isn't involved in a part of the woman's life, look at how much of their life they do share. Take time to examine and recognize all the reference points that do matter. Did I mention that our fellow and the aunt go over to our young woman's house to watch the kids so she and her husband can go out on a date?

Have you ever had conversations in which someone was practicing one-upmanship? You tell a story of something your kids got into and the problem it caused, and then they tell you a counter-story that exceeds yours in degree or scope. "My kids got out the cereal box and opened it up and spilled it all over the kitchen floor." "Oh, that's nothing, my youngest two got a 5-pound bag of flour and trailed it through the dining room, up the steps and dumped it all over themselves, my bed and my bedroom. It was a flour (dust) cloud." (True story!)

Bonding

The reason many of us tell stories of events and travails is to share our experiences. We involve others in our lives and give them a peek, or snapshot, of who we are and what we have been through or are going through. Generally, they shake their heads in knowing agreement, and/or then proceed to commiserate with us by informing us of a similar story that pertains to their life or, at the very least, someone they know. Other times we share as understanding partners in the human drama, to let you know that your experience, while perhaps unique to you, is not isolated to you. The usual un-admitted and unacknowledged inclination is to generally elevate your mood and lift your spirit by showing and revealing to you that they have experienced this part of your life, either previously or right now. Sharing experiences has the benefit of informing and instructing through information and, more importantly, raising hopes in the reality that we are not alone in our experiences... others have been there and done that! Yet a person may feel and say, "I understand what you are saying, but it doesn't help anyway."

I said usually un-admitted and unacknowledged inclination, but not always. Sometimes when we are having these conversations we truthfully may say, "I'm just trying to help." We may use that phrase and say that truth in response to someone's resistance to our help. We're trying to reassure them of our motives and build them up in the downcast of their souls. In lighter occasions we are trying to build camaraderie. Commonality pulls people together. Shared experiences bond people. Being on the same bowling team. Rooting for the same football team. Being involved in the same line of work naturally provokes conversation related to that line of work. Doctors can relate to other doctors easier and truck drivers relate to other truck drivers, as would a soldier to a soldier. There is nothing inherently wrong with this. These things, and many more identity factors, bring, pull, and bond people one to another. Yet, there is one bonding mechanism that triggers closeness rapidly and that is adversity. Yes, adversity.

Together In Adversity

Adversity (From dictionary reference.com)

1. Adverse fortune or fate; a condition marked by misfortune, calamity, or distress: *A friend will show his or her true colors in times of adversity.*

2. An adverse or unfortunate event or circumstance: *You will meet many adversities in life.*

All you must do is observe the general population's reaction(s) to adversity. Witness a nation after a terrorist attack on its homeland; an attack on one is an attack on all. Suddenly, so many differences were automatically dispelled by the more immediate bond of "We are under attack." Notice the use of "we" which signifies the unity of us, one nation.

Occurring more regionally when a community must face weather-related issues. When the floodwaters rise. When the tornado rips through. When the earthquake tremors finally die down. When the drought continues. The people of a region have that as a shared experience and use that phrase as a sign of unity. The experience becomes unifying, and then begins the stories of how the citizenry helped each other. How a population overcame. The news reports and newspaper articles tell the tales of involvement. Word spreads of good deeds performed. Adversity comes to larger groups, such as nations and states, right on down to smaller groups, churches, families, and neighborhoods. How people pull together for one another, for the benefit of one another, is what bonds and unifies and is also what builds lasting relationships.

Think about how churches pull together when it comes time for a church expansion program or a building project.

Or how a church pulls together if they are the victims of arson. One example, a church was the victim of flooding and other churches, not even of the same denomination yet in the same community, gave monetary gifts to help them out. Neighborhoods pull together for block parties, crime watches, and for their local school sports teams. Something we come together for with the purpose of achieving a goal and/or overcoming an obstacle and then we can refer to that past event as what forged new relationships, because there was an understanding that we were in it together.

The Identity Of Us (We)

Look at the understandable tightening of a family unit when adversity strikes. When the doctor reports that someone in the family now has a hardcore illness, our family unit feels threatened because, if one of our own is threatened, then we are also. They are part of what we are a part of...the family. The family members are alerted, spiritual tension rises, and internal alarm mechanisms are sounded due to the truth that it's one of us. It is the "us" that is threatened. You see, the "us" is an identity. So, when one of "us" is threatened, then what is under attack is an identity. The common identity that is recognized as "We" or the identity of "Us." It doesn't matter who makes up the "We" or "Us," if there are people who recognize "We" or "Us" as an identity.

That identity comes in various configurations, and it certainly comes from many perspectives. The identity of "We/Us" can be recognized as a husband, wife and two children. The identity of "Us" can be Mom and Dad, daughter and son-in-law, one grandson and a son in college. It can extend to grandparents. It may mean nothing but siblings. The identity of "Us" may just mean husband and wife. The configurations vary.

The perspective of "Us" depends on from whose viewpoint the identity of "Us" is being referenced. The husband may, at some point or for specific reasons, see the identity of "Us" as only he and his wife - - for perhaps when setting budgets, considering volume of children, or where to retire. The husband, at some other point, may consider the identity of "Us" more inclusively to include his children, in-laws and grandchildren when planning for a Christmas holiday get-together. If family reunions are forthcoming, then the configuration and perspective of the identity of "Us" takes on an even more expansive meaning. The identity of "Us" can expand or contract within the mind of the individual based on their own criteria.

If one of us is facing a health issue, the rest of us, while feeling our identity threatened, still recognize that it is the "one" (out of "us") who is most directly threatened, but the focus is not for the one to experience it alone. When anyone feels isolated, they may lose hope perhaps not even apply themselves to the extent that is needed to endure, if they apply themselves at all. Sometimes they adopt an attitude which perceives the situation as one of punishment or even a time of penance. Now we acknowledge the law of sowing and reaping...sometimes we are going through something that truly is of our own making.

Considering this idea of punishment, or penance, within the prison system. If an inmate has behavior that is out of line with the rules, one of the corrective or penal methods employed by the authorities is to put that prisoner in solitary confinement. In other words, in isolation. Removing that individual from human contact intentionally is a method to penalize the violation or correct the behavior. The anticipation is that by removing them from others, they will immediately cease to be a threat to established order and become an example to others for similar infractions. Hopefully, remedial in that period of isolation, is suffering by being alone which is punitive in nature. Because of not wanting to be in isolation again, the prisoner will meet the norms desired. Think also of when a child is behaving in a way not tolerable. One practice many parents choose is the good old-fashioned "stand in the corner or go to your room." Going to your room nowadays may not be such a great idea if there's a computer, iPad, or television to be utilized, let alone a smart phone for texting friends, etc. For younger children standing alone in a corner, where all can see you, may be more imposing as a discipline measure and therefore more effective. Even though others surround you, walk past you, and you can hear their dialogue, you are still alone in this discipline, this suffering, this isolation. Remarkable how you are not alone in population, yet you are alone in your situation...at least in the unique moment of standing in the corner.

So, it goes with some people who, even though others are around them in the identity of "Us," may still believe and feel alone, isolated, and in solitary confinement.

No One Understands What I'm Going Through!

From that mentality starts the vocal arousal of "Why me? What have I done? I feel like no one understands what I'm going through!" Even when others bring reassurance to you that you are part of an identity of "Us," some believe that they are standing in the corner by themselves. Taken to another level perhaps the perspective has now elevated, or lowered itself to, "I'm in solitary confinement." Thoughts go forth like, "What did I do to deserve this? No one else cares! I'm enduring this with no one else." Sometimes these ideas are reinforced with the introverted expressions of "You may sympathize with me, or have compassion toward me, but you really don't understand what I'm going through. Yes, you may say you understand, but you still have your job, I don't. I'm the one who was downsized, not you. I'm the one on unemployment, not you. I'm the one who must start over after the divorce, not you."

"You may say you understand but you still have reasonable health. I'm the one diagnosed with cancer, not you. You are not the one who must go through chemo, I am. You are not the one who must take insulin every day, I do. You are not the one who must endure physical therapy every day because of the accident, I am. You still have your marriage, I don't. I just lost my parent, you didn't. It's my kids who are on drugs, not yours."

The list and thought patterns roll on, "But I can feel what's going on right now." I may show you some surface gratitude because social etiquette demands it, but deep down, I'm screaming. "Does anyone understand what I'm going through?" What speaks to me is someone who has lived out this reality and can justifiably relate to me. The one who really understands is someone who has had to go through what I'm going through. If not in practice, or literally, then at least in principle, they have commonality with me."

From that perspective, we are looking for an identity of "Us." "We have been through this, and we will get through this!" No one wants to be standing in the corner alone, or in isolation, especially when they have done nothing substantial, if anything at all, in bringing on their situation. Unfortunately, everyone at some time or another refuses or resists the recognition of those around us who are trying to identify with us. While we don't want to be in isolation, something triggers inside of us that sees our situation as isolated. Our perspective, our outlook, and our attitude mesh to the real or imagined place that we are alone in some respect if for no other reason than "No one understands what I am going through! Who could possibly understand or feel my soul? Only I can feel my soul. Know my thoughts. Have my feelings. Who can relate to me?"

While believing oneself isolated may be a little bit contemptuous of life, the individual continues sometimes in a self-imposed martyrdom of struggle. A victim of their own making or delusion. Sometimes not...what happens when an individual has a correct diagnosis of their isolation? The reality of some type of social solitude? "Who is with me? Whom can I turn to for sustenance? Support? Help? Understanding?" Then comes either the big recommendation by those around you or the thought you think on your own, turn to God!

Turn To God?

On the surface, for most, it has a soothing appeal. "God is God. He knows all things. He's all powerful. He sees all things." A person usually has intellectual assent to these attributes of God, but skepticism can find a home in an individual going through challenges. That skepticism can be paired to cynicism. The person's emotions take precedence in all considerations, including the involvement of God. They may believe that God isn't truly interested in what they are going through, and the primary reason is because of God's lack of experience. God may see it. He may know all about our situation like a newspaper article or documentary. God may even feel certain emotions or sympathies toward our circumstances, much like the typical person's reaction would be toward someone involved in an accident, but the question that plagues us is this, "Does God really understand what I'm going through?"

The train of thought that directs our outlook on this situation is derived from the teaching of God being transcendent which simplistically means that God is above it all. Or even that God is removed from the situation; that God is separate from the world and man. One erroneous aspect of this thinking is that God can't be bothered by us and our condition because God has bigger and more important things to do, like run the universe and deal with the spiritual world and the human race as a whole so as not to get caught up in one individual's struggle.

The thinking continues, "What If God starts to bother with us and gets distracted from other responsibilities? Can God multi-task? What if God has so many other prayer requests and concerns that I'm on this big spiritual waiting list and by the time he gets to me it will be too late? If God can't be bothered with me, does that mean he is too busy or is it that God prefers it to be that way because, deep down, he is cold and uncaring? Maybe God isn't cold and uncaring, just distant and indifferent. Kind of like, "You people are on your own; just do the best you can." Does God want me to quit praying because it's like the phone going off and interrupting your business? Are there so many prayer requests going up to Heaven that a bunch of angels are acting as air traffic controllers trying to get some prayers to land? Or are the angels trying to sort out and prioritize the prayer requests by importance, or by whom they and God like the most? And if I'm not in the club, then I must get in line behind "the favorites." Since I'm barely on the radar, I can never move up the prayer line because someone else keeps cutting in."

Is God the beleaguered parent who has too many kids and can't keep up with us all? Perhaps the idea of transcendence taken too far is that God is unreachable, but then that takes away from God's being all-knowing, which is the word "Omniscient." If God is all-knowing, then he knows about me, he knows about my situation, he has all the facts and information like a well-informed God should.

Many times, people believe that they are in one place and God is in another. Intellectually God is "in the know" about their situation but he is more like an observing God than an involved God. This outlook has God in the position of perhaps being apathetic, uncaring, or inactive, limited in power or willpower, and that makes him impotent or weak. If God knows something, but doesn't do something, or won't do something, then that rationale leads us to conclude God's not being all-powerful; this is the word

"Omnipotent." If God is omnipotent, all-powerful, then he should flex his spiritual muscle and come to my aid. Doesn't that line of thinking interfere with God's omniscience, or all-knowing attribute? If God is all-knowing, then he should know when and how to be all-powerful or when and how to not be all-powerful.

Including God In "We"

This isn't really the crux of our problem. Most people don't necessarily want or even need someone to fix their situation. They just want someone to understand them and to go through it with them. They don't want to stand in the corner alone or to be in isolation. They want to establish and maintain some form of identity of "Us." They want and need someone to be there with them and quite honestly, most people want to know that God is there, and they want him to be part of the identity of "Us." That "We" …and "we" includes God…are going through this together. The proper perspective of God being transcendent, or above it all, isn't that he is removed, apathetic, uncaring, or aloof; it's that he is not affected in a negative way by our circumstances. He is not going to stop being God to the universe, to others, or to you. That still doesn't answer the soul-searching and spiritually deep question, "Does God really understand what I'm going through?"

For someone to typically be supportive of what you are

going through, they need to be near the situation. If not physically close then at least available in a communicative way, such as phone conversations, E-mail and so forth. But the attribute of God being separated from and removed from us in the teaching of his transcendence does injustice to his love and compassion when it is not balanced with the teaching of an attribute of God called his "Immanence;" this simply means his presence and nearness in the world and to man. At Christmastime many sing the carol "O Come, O Come, Emmanuel." "Emmanuel" means "God with us" so God's immanence means his closeness and his presence with us. How many have heard the scripture from Psalm 23:4 (NIV), "Even though I walk through the valley of the shadow of death, I will fear no evil for you are with me"? Many scriptures are quoted and prayed to give us reassurance that God is with us. Transcendence, God separated from it all, and Immanence, God's nearness to it all, are not in contradiction. They are attributes of God that complement one another. One reveals God's superiority and sovereignty; the other simultaneously conveys his concern and attention to our lives.

There are people in our lives who are close to our situation. They may or may not have a vested interest in what we are going through; it all depends on the involvement level they have in our lives. I believe the same can be said of God, to a great degree. While God is close to everyone's situation (Immanence), what is his involvement level in our life? People can be close to our situation in that they know details, have the facts, have the chronological history all put together and intimately understand all the parties in the situation; but their involvement level is next to nothing, or nothing, because we don't want that person's participation or have not thought to ask for that person's contribution to our situation. Have we asked others for their inclusion, and have we asked God to become involved? To involve anyone else may include informing them. As it concerns God, because he is omniscient, all-knowing, he is already informed. Generally, we must issue an invitation by dialoguing with others, bringing them closer by conversation and continuing their involvement. Do we dialogue with God? In other words, do we pray? The bottom line--do we talk to God? God wants us to talk to him. Just because someone may know the facts doesn't mean that they are participating in our situation. If I never talk to you about what I'm going through, even though you may know the facts, my silence toward you possibly says that I don't want you to be involved. Maybe my pride stands in the way, and I don't want to ask for help.

Our encouragement factors are - - God is omnipotent, all-powerful, and omniscient, all-knowing. He has the wisdom of when to use his power and when not to, even for our situation. He knows what needs to be done and what needs to happen; what shouldn't be done and what shouldn't happen. and the power and means to accomplish same. God is close to us. He is only a prayer away from involvement. We talk to him, thereby establishing and continuing with the identity of "Us" with God being part of the "Us." This includes individuals, couples, families, communities, nations, and whatever configurations and perspectives of the identity of "Us" that there are.

In our circumstance, now someone -- in this case, God -- is involved. At this juncture, we settle beyond the notion of God's involvement into the faith reality of God's presence. Yet there is one resistance factor that some of us employ in our faith reality, especially as it concerns God. Some would rationalize that certainly God has complete functional knowledge of our situation. He knows all the mechanics and dynamics. While he may even have a certain amount of sympathy, compassion and even pity, God can't truly empathize with us in the sense of having experiential understanding because he has not been through what we are going through or what others have gone through. Intellectually God has got it all together but unless he's "been there, done that and bought the T-shirt," we still have some sort of disconnect with him. Many appreciate experience as a factor in relating to one another. We can believe that God loves us, cares about us, knows the facts about us, can help us, yet we disappointingly may think or believe that because God hasn't lived it personally, he really doesn't understand it. The experience factor on God's part in this identity of "Us" is missing. Of course, we appreciate his involvement, and we feel his presence in our faith reality, but in this relationship, we believe we are the frontrunners in the area of experiences. Just because we're close to a person and involved in their situation doesn't mean we can truly understand it if we have not lived it ourselves. That in no way implies a lack of concern, or lack of love and compassion, and the tears shed are real. The hope offered is genuine. The advice given comes with the best of intentions. but in adversity, the "We" who are going through a situation has, as an extra reinforcement mechanism, the "common shared experience" as the essence of the identity factors in relating to one another.

Can We Relate To God Or Him To Us?

While God loves us, cares about us, wants to be involved and we want him involved; if he hasn't been through what we've been through or hasn't lived what we have gone through, then the question remains, "Does God really understand what I'm going through?"

Can he relate to us in a way that satisfies the human urge to have common shared experiences that are the "icing on the cake" of the identity of "Us?" Can we relate to someone who doesn't even have a street address? It's not that we don't get along, and, by all means, we agree with his agenda, his ideas and ideals, but it isn't like God's lying-in bed at night elbowing the one who keeps stealing the covers. Let's face facts, God doesn't have to ever worry about getting the kids to school on time, running out of milk, or dirty laundry. The last we knew, God never had to apply for a job. (I wonder what the résumé would look like. Who would be his references? What work experience would he refer to? What kind of background check could we do?

How can we relate to someone who doesn't have to balance a budget or worry about his 401K? He never catches a cold! In so many ways, we are worlds apart from each other as it concerns the life experiences of, we humans and the life experiences of God. I never created the Heavens and the Earth; I can't even create a good-looking garden. He laid out the stars in the sky; it's an effort for me to correctly make the bed. God sits on Heaven's throne and I'm trying to get one promotion before retirement. God has walked on water, and I can't even roller skate. While I'm having some difficulty in coming to terms with God not being able to relate to me, I guess there is some degree to which I can't relate to him. God doesn't have needs or issues; I do. God is self-sufficient, I'm not and you are not. For someone to understand and relate to needs and issues, they must have experienced needs and had issues. What kind of experience does God have in what I have gone through or am going through?

This book is about revealing that God really does understand what we are going through because, either in practice or principle, he has "been there, done that, and bought the T-shirt." God has experienced in a practical way...literally, in some cases...what we experience. What God has not experienced literally; he has experienced in principle. Remember the word "Emmanuel? which means "God with us?" Its immediate reference is to the fact that God came to us as a human being. He was born a human, raised as a human, lived as a human, died as a human. With that reality, combined with he being the eternal God, he has experienced and continues to experience the human drama as it was and is lived by him. God does relate to our situations.

The short and sweet answer is "Yes, God really does understand what I'm going through." He understands what each human is going through. All our pains, struggles, valleys, frustrations, temptations, and the list goes on. God understands relationships and the different configurations and perspectives of the identities of "Us." He can relate to every emotion we can exhibit. In the pages that follow, I will detail in practice or principle that we have a God who truly isn't just compassionate and sympathetic, but also empathetic. He is connected to us by common shared experiences. What other belief system or religion can make this claim?

The proof is in the scripture as recorded evidence. We

will look at the substantial facts laid out before us in plain sight. As we travel through the Bible, studying different categories of the human experience, the anticipation is that we will have a deeper appreciation for what he went through and that our relationship with him as individuals, couples and other identities of "We" will be enhanced by the reality of God relating to us and us to him. Our God is not removed from us. He has intimately lived out our lives and he continue to live out our lives.

Like Him, Like Us

How many even think of the fact that God has emotions and an emotional range? You will see where God experiences anger, frustration, disappointment, sorrow, hope and joy. How God went through betrayal, injustice, rejection, and desertion. I will exhibit examples of God victimized by adultery. The target of conspiracy and court injustice. Someone who faced the death penalty. God as an individual who has had family problems and went through a church split. He has been the bullied and then beaten-up. The object of scorn and ridicule. On the other side of that spectrum, he lived as someone who could hardly get any peace because of his celebrity. He knows what it is to face death. He understands a work ethic, organizing people and leadership. He knows what it is to submit to authority. God faced office politics, workgroup issues, and providing for others. He also was basically homeless even though he had a hometown. He felt thirst, hunger, and pain, both physical and emotional. God has even cried. He had parents, siblings, friends, enemies, and followers.

On one hand. he is the creator of the universe and holds everything together by his power; on the other hand, he came as one of us and went through life subordinating himself to our lives. The obvious, number-one reason was so that he could die like one of us (a human experience) and take away our sins as we accept him as Lord and Savior. Another reason was so that we could see the great love and empathy he has toward us. Since he came and experienced life, it should leave us with no disconnects or disappointments in his ability to relate to and understand whatever it is that we are going through. We have the reassurances of common, shared experiences. The quintessence of the identity factors. However, ingrained our outlook on God's transcendence may be, this book seeks to educate with the balance of his Immanence; His nearness to our situation and his closeness isn't just because of the factual information that God has, but his closeness is punctuated by his ability to identify with us. We referenced God's omnipotence (all-powerfulness), God's omniscience (all-knowingness), but there is also God's omnipresence which is defined as God everywhere at once. Not just up in Heaven, but also right here, right now, with you, everyone, everywhere, all the time, and at the same time. I believe that God is also Omni-experienced. That he has or is experiencing everything we are or have, in the past, in practice and or principle. In the present, literally and in real time. This book will devote much of its attention to the past but will provide room for the experience of the here and now, the literal and real-time Omni-experience of God.

When you are done reading, understanding, and relating to the information provided; when you assimilate into your soul and spirit this concept, you will never ask again "Does God really understand what I'm going through?"

Chapter 2

Does God Really Understand The Loss Of A Loved One?

Out of all the things that we humans go through, one of the hardest issues we must face is the loss of a loved one. It is considered inherently as a hardcore experience. The felt emotion is of loss. Something and someone are no longer available. They are no longer with us, and the identity of we, or us, has been violated, and broken." Done away with," literally, only to live on in memory. What was, no longer is, and will not be again. The relationship of the other person can't be experienced anymore. They are not here for conversation. They are not here for familiarity, closeness or attachment. The loss caused by death has meaning. The relationship mattered, but does everyone's death matter to you? The honest reality is, of course not! If you lose something that you don't value, there is no sense of loss. If you lose some pocket change, typically you would shrug your shoulders and get on with life. But if you lost a roll of hundred-dollar bills, a nasty gut wrench would occur. Obviously, there was greater value of the one over the other. Even if some old family pictures were destroyed, they may not be worth much commercially, but the nostalgic value and emotional worth that they hold, could send some into a tizzy over the loss. You see, there is no sense of loss, if there is no sense of value. The greater the sense of value that something, or someone holds, determines the degree to which you feel the loss. Witness the sense of loss when a President or other great public figure dies, especially if it is considered an untimely death...something that should not have happened yet. A nation mourns and remembers. That person was valued; the relationship they had with the people of a nation has been broken. When someone we value dies, there is an immense loss and the more valued the relationship, the greater the sense or feel of that loss. The loss of a spouse is felt much deeper than the loss of a cousin whom you see only at family reunions. The value we place on the loss of relationships is not necessarily what that relationship should have been, but what it really was. Next, let's look at two biblical stories for some insight into the thought of, and the value of, relationships as they really were. The norms tailored and tempered by reality.

The Value of a Relationship

At this they wept again. Then Orpah kissed

> *her mother-in-law good-by, but Ruth clung to her. "Look," said Naomi, "Your sister-in-law is going back to her people and her gods. Go back with her." but Ruth replied, "Don't urge me to leave you or to turn back from you. Where you go, I will go, and where you stay, I will stay. Your people will be my people and your God my God." "Where you die, I will die, and there I will be buried. May the Lord deal with me, be it ever so severely, if anything but death separates you and me." When Naomi realized that Ruth was determined to go with her, she stopped urging her.*
>
> Ruth 1:14-18

We see in this story that Ruth was the daughter-in-law of Naomi and she refused to abandon that relationship, even when the death of her husband no longer kept her as a daughter-in-law. Naomi released her to go back to her original family, but Ruth was so bonded to Naomi, that she refused to give up her relationship, except when death would occur. This isn't the norm. Overwhelmingly, most daughters by marriage would not trek off with their mother-in-law to a foreign land under these circumstances. Yet Ruth had developed an attachment to Naomi that was valued over everything else at that point. The relationship wasn't what most would think it to be; it was greater, demonstrating its intensity and value.

> *When Athaliah the mother of Ahaziah saw that her son was dead; she proceeded to destroy*

> *the whole royal family. But Jehosheba, the daughter of King Jehoram and sister of Ahaziah, took Joash son of Ahaziah and stole him away from among the royal princes, who were about to be murdered. She put him and his nurse in a bedroom to hide him from Athaliah so he was not killed. He remained hidden with his nurse at the temple of the Lord for six years while Athaliah ruled the land.*
> 2 Kings 11:1-3

Athaliah sought to destroy her own family. Joash was her grandson. As the relationship should be, Athaliah would at the very least hold onto the royal seat until her grandson was old enough to take over. She would mentor him along the way, have him tutored and educated by the nation's finest to prepare him for his future, and then have him seated at an appropriate time. But alas, Grandma had other ideas! Kill everyone off, including the grandkids so that she could have the throne all to herself. Reasonable people would have to admit, that is not the way this relationship should be, but it was reality. She placed no value on her relationship with her family. In fact, she was responsible for their demise. But with Athaliah, there was no sense of loss, because there was no sense of value. Since she didn't value them and the relationships, she could withstand the loss. Again, not as it should be, but as it really was.

Death, in a nutshell, is separation. Death separates the soul and spirit from the physical body. That's what happens to the individual that dies. What happens relationally to us when they die, or separate, is that we are separated from continuing the relationship. Not only us, but everyone else that had some type of relationship with the person who died or separated. When we lose someone, people come to the funeral service, which is a type of memorial to the person, and pay their respects. This is honoring the value, of the relationships that person had, and gives condolences to the sense of loss, due to the death. We put up picture displays, memorabilia, give out words of honor, and gather to conduct a service in honor of the value of the relationship. Let's look at another relationship that had value.

A Valued Relationship

This is my son, whom I love. With him I am well pleased.
                                                    Matthew 3:17

This is my son, whom I love, with him I am well pleased. Listen to him.
                                                    Matthew 17:5

Jesus gave them this answer: "I tell you the truth, the Son can do nothing by himself: he can do only what he sees his Father doing, because whatever the Father does the Son also does. For the Father loves the Son and shows him all he does. Yes, to your amazement he will show him even greater things than these. For just as the

Father raises the dead and gives them life; even so the Son gives life to whom he is pleased to give it. Moreover, the Father judges no one, but has entrusted all judgment to the Son, that all may honor the Son just as they honor the father. He who does not honor the Son does not honor the Father, who sent him."
John 5:19-23

Especially note verse 20 where it reads, "The Father loves the Son." In reviewing Matthew 3:17 and Matthew 17:5 both state "My son." The first thing to establish here is the position of belonging... "My son" ...we see they are related. There is a Father and Son relationship that God himself is recognizing and affirming. He is saying that Jesus Christ belongs to him, just like any other Father would say of their son. Both verses continue to read, "whom I love." This just wasn't for the ears of his Son; he was informing others also of his feelings towards his Son. The Father wasn't just pointing out to others of the relationship; he also wanted everyone to know of his attachment. The obvious reality is, God the Father has a Son, whom he loves and he's not ashamed to admit it nor embarrassed to reveal that fact. He openly confesses the value of the relationship, but it doesn't end there. He continues by adding, "With him I am well pleased." It's a good thing to admit the value of relationships. In and of itself, most parents love and value their children, even if they don't get along that well. There is a bond that is there naturally despite whatever differences there may be between parents and their children. Yet, in looking at these statements, we find that the Father also says, "With him I am well pleased." What he is revealing is that there are no issues between them; everything's going great; they were getting along. How many parents can say the same thing?" With my child I am well pleased." Not just "I'm okay with the direction they are taking in life." Not just tolerating the decisions they are making but approving of them. To further the thought, it wasn't just a positive nod that was cast in his son's direction, but he said, "well pleased." When we examine John 5:19-23, we see that the Father had involved the Son in his affairs. Verse 20 reveals they were a team. There is a sense of partnership and even promotion for the son. This relationship is characterized by trust and mutual respect (verse 23). Every decent parent wants a good relationship with their children. God the Father has an excellent relationship with his Son, I would even say perfect. There is a family connection; they were a family unit. There is recorded life and value to this father and son relationship. The truth is, this is the way it really was and still is.

In answering the question, "Does God really understand what I'm going through," some of the questions are: Does God really understand death, the loss of a loved one? Does God really understand what it is to lose someone you love, or to watch them die? Can he identify with that kind of pain or hurt? Remember, the sense of loss is tied to the value of what was lost. We have proven the relationship and its value of God the Father and God the Son. Next let's read further selections from scripture, Matthew 27:50, "Gave up his spirit." Mark 15:37 "Breathed his last." Luke 23:46 "He breathed his last." John 19:30 (he) "bowed his head and gave up his spirit." All four Gospels record the death of Jesus Christ; they record his separation from God, his father.

Losing A Loved One

There is no way to escape the inevitable conclusion that the Father had just lost his son. Being omniscient (all knowing), and omnipresent (everywhere at the same time), he also saw his son die! God just lost his child! There was a death in the family. Many people suffer through the loss of a loved one, but most would agree that the most painful loss is of a child. There's unnaturalness about a child dying before its parents. It is a grief and hurt from which some never really recover. We can bear up from most relational losses, but the loss of a child is a separation, a death that stays with us longer than other losses. God didn't just lose a loved one, he felt and experienced the most painful category of loss, a child. To top it off, it was his son whom he loved and was well pleased. The Father experienced this very personally. He went through it himself. It was his only son, his only child, his only begotten. God understands death, the loss of a loved one. He's "been there and done that." A Father saw his only child die and that Father was, and is, God himself.

At this point, detractors may try to point out that since circumstances may differ which might make the loss different. Some truthfully could claim "my child died in a vehicle accident, yours didn't." Others could say that their child died of an illness, perhaps cancer or from accidents. First, let's lay a foundation. It is not the age of the child that makes it hurtful any more or any less. The 65-year-old parents who had a 40-year-old child die from a vehicle accident, cancer, etc., feels no less grief, pain, or sense of loss if they valued the relationship, than the 30-year-old parents that losses a 5-year-old. Some may declare that the way or the reason that someone dies, in this case, a child, makes it more traumatic. The point of God, or anyone for that matter, experiencing loss, is not the circumstances of the death. It's not the fact of causation that led to the loss of a loved one, it's the principle of the heartache and pain of the loss. God understands what it is to lose a loved one, even and especially a child, and he can truly empathize and bring comfort as someone who has gone through what you are going through. Not in exact circumstances, perhaps, but for certain in principle.

This brings up some interesting thoughts on this form of dialogue. What were the circumstances that God the Father had to endure in the issue of his Son's death?

Watching It Happen

How many parents have watched their children treated unfairly? Their own child, being the victim of some type of injustice, whether at the hands of their peers in the category of bullies, or in the workplace as they may be treated unfairly, or in the court system that was supposed to have given them justice and failed. There are documented stories of war crimes committed against others, gross mistreatment by humans against humans. Way too often, this mistreatment leads to someone's death. That someone is someone's child, no matter their age. Government soldiers or guards, beating, harassing, and victimizing their prisoners, often with the approval of the authorities. What did God the Father witness and what did he feel during those hours? What he felt was what any decent loving parent would feel. What he witnessed was what no parent should ever have to see. Matthew 26:3-4, "Then the chief priests and the elders of the people assembled in the palace of the high priest, whose name was Caiaphas, and they plotted to arrest Jesus in some sly way and kill him." Matthew 26:59-60, "the chief priests and the whole Sanhedrin were looking for false evidence against Jesus so that they could put him to death. But they did not find any, though many false witnesses came forward."

Here we see the fact of conspiracy, and not just a conspiracy to make someone look bad in front of the boss;

not just one disgruntled coworker or a couple of fellow workers. This wasn't a run in with the local zoning officer either. Here we have the issue of a conspiracy by a large group in authority; religious people included, who plotted beyond trying to besmirch his good reputation. The plot wasn't intended to stop at giving Jesus a criminal record to handicap any potential public ambitions. It was a plot to make sure he got the death penalty! These weren't drug dealers and embezzlers; these were supposed to be the vanguards of society. The protectors of order; the leadership of a nation. It wasn't that they were looking for juicy gossip that might have had some truth attached to it, nor they were merely looking to dig up some dirt from his past. There were not any skeletons in his closet. The conspiracy included as part of its plan, the intention to lie, and now, the victimization would include a frame up. A frame up with intention on the death penalty. How many people have watched their children become pawns in this type of power struggle? How many parents have seen their child taken into custody unjustly, treated inhumanly, and then insulted and mocked in a kangaroo court with a predetermined guilty sentence?

> *Then they spit in his face and struck him with their fists. Others slapped him and said, "Prophesy to us, Christ. Who hit you?"*
> Matthew 26:67-68

Then some began to spit at him; they blindfolded

him, struck him with their fists, and said, "Prophesy!" And the guards took him and beat him.
Mark 14:65

Then Pilate took Jesus and had him flogged. The soldiers twisted together a crown of thorns and put it on his head. They clothed him in a purple robe and went up to him again and again, saying, "Hail, king of the Jews!" And they struck him in the face.
John 19:1-3

All parents cringe when they see their child hurt. No matter if they are 3 years old and fell and scrapped their knees, or 10 years old and fell off their bike. 20 years old and banged up in a car accident. 40 years old and hurt their back at work. There are different levels of being hurt and different degrees of pain. There are also different types of pain. The emotional pain of when your child is teased at school, taunted at the sports game, put down at work. In these examples, The Father watched his son get spit on, slapped, punched, flogged (whipped), struck in the face, humiliated, mocked, and insulted. This was basically the prelude to even worse. Most parents would bristle at that type of mistreatment over anyone, let alone their own child. How infuriated you would become. Would not your heart bleed and you'd cry out, "Stop! Enough physical abuse! Enough emotional abuse! My son is an innocent man. He has never been in trouble. His whole life was dedicated to doing well for others. Look at the life he has led. It is a life filled with healing. Devoted to loving and forgiving. He has given hope to the hopeless. Are you people insane? Who in their right mind could find fault with such a life as the one he has lived? And it's not enough that the leadership is against him, but now they turn the people against him also?"

> *Now it was the governor's custom at the Feast to release a prisoner chosen by the crowd. At that time they had a notorious prisoner, called Barabbas. So when the crowd had gathered, Pilate asked them, "Which one do you want me to release to you: Barabbas, or Jesus who is called the Messiah?" For he knew it was out of self-interest that they had handed Jesus over to him. But the chief priests and the elders persuaded the crowd to ask for Barabbas and to have Jesus executed.*
> Matthew 27:15-18, 20

Would we examine this scenario and think to ourselves, how many people in this crowd that are shouting "crucify him" had at some point in their lives been touched by his life? How many of them had been healed? How many of their own relatives or children had he healed and set free? Perhaps your thoughts would be, "but now they are turning against my son, and they are trading him for a notorious prisoner. What ingratitude!" At this point, how many of us would be thinking or wishing that our son would have never gotten involved and done so much good for the many who are so ungrateful? To top it off, they aren't just rejecting his leadership, or his offer of help; they are actively promoting the death penalty for his son and the persuasion from the conspirators was too much.

Who has experienced being present at the cruelty done to their child? Who among humanity has witnessed their own child's travails? Most have never seen their offspring shot, stabbed, beaten, or mutilated, yet God the Father witnessed his child being tortured. Some get the news from the police, by a knock on the door, that their child has died. God the Father watched as the criminal (in) justice system helped perpetuate this victimization. Others rally to the bedside of their dying child and conduct vigils. God the Father witnessed his Son's crucifixion on the cross. He saw the circumstances of his son's death, and deathbed. The false witness and conspiracy. The physical and emotional abuse. The turning of public opinion. God the Father watched his son get murdered. The victim of a crime and the cover up. He watched him die slowly, on a cross, bleeding in pain; an innocent man suffering through no fault of his own.

To add the proverbial insult to injury, who showed up at the funeral? Where were the thousands that he had fed? Where were the thousands that he had healed and given deliverance? Where were all the people that he had taught and blessed? Where were the crowds that thronged to hear his parables? Where was the honor due to him and where were his closest associates, his disciples?" They traded my son for some loser named Barabbas!"

It usually doesn't make obvious sense when we lose loved ones, especially under tragic circumstances, such as what Jesus experienced. Our general outlook is to perceive the loss as worse if the death is occurring in youth, or if our loved one had no contributing factors to their own death. The difference could be looked at as this: In a first scenario, you have our first person, a young adult, who goes out drinking, becomes extremely intoxicated, and then drives far above the speed limit, loses control of the vehicle, runs through a red light, smashes into another vehicle and consequently dies. In the second scenario, you have a young adult who simply goes out to run a few errands and is driving sensibly but is smashed into by the first person and also dies. As a society, in general, our sympathies would be more directed towards the second person because we would rightfully discern that they did nothing wrong, and since they did nothing wrong, the usual thoughts are that they didn't deserve to die. Since they didn't deserve it, then it was unfair for them to die. How many would speak out and say that a child's death, no matter the age, wasn't fair. The Father can clearly say that it wasn't fair for his child to die either! We would proclaim, "They shouldn't have died!" but neither should have Jesus died by any broken law or wrongdoing. The Father understands this kind of injustice and thought-life pattern.

The "If's And If Only's"

There are many heart-wrenching questions in those situations; there are also many types of "what if's" and "if only' s." What if the first person wouldn't have been drinking? What if the second person would have been just a little bit sooner or later in passing through? As we go over and over the circumstances again and again, we can keep repeating the same "what if's" and "if only's," as a temporary and imaginary consolation to loss and pain. The "what if's" and "if only's" become alternative reality escapism to help prepare us for final acceptance. Yet, still, years after our loss, we may continue to indulge the "ifs" because of what we wished had been instead of what really occurred. It is a coping mechanism; the melancholy of the "if's."

The typical question that marches to the forefront in any untimely or tragic death is "Why?" We ask in the belief that if we only knew the answer, it would help us deal with the loss. The first thing in the ability to deal with something is to be able to understand it. If we don't understand it, frustration sets in." Why did this happen?" "Why did they die?" Some phrase it "Why did they have to die?" We ask with the connotation that if someone died for a purpose, for a just cause, that even while the same hurt and pain would be present, at least there was rationale. It makes acceptance a little easier. We are looking for meaning, or in truth, for answers. We ask hoping that some truth will dawn in our souls. Maybe someone will become enlightened and share with us that knowledge. Yet intuitively, most of us realize that an omniscient God knows why. Hence the end of the line of questioning begins, "Why God?" Or more directly, and sometimes accusatorially, "Why did God let this happen?"

Why, God?

In our hurt and anger, we say many things that we would never otherwise say. In our hurt and anger, we are thinking many things that we normally don't think. That thinking leads to speaking. We seek to somehow appease our felt emotions. Our emotions, or feelings, are not pleasant so we seek remediation of those feelings to find a more tolerable level. When that tolerable level can't be achieved in our breaking point timeframes, then the release mechanism becomes expressed verbally as "soul salve," however shallow or wrong that may be. Sometimes, due to thinking which becomes abnormal in its logic or self-centered for perceived sanity checks and balances, we rationalize viewpoints that may become abnormal. If the starting point is wrong, then the ending point usually is also wrong.

One of the end results which manifest itself from the emotions of hurt and pain and can't find "soul salve," is the "blame game." The "blame game" can also find itself birthed from the alliance of the "what if's" and the "if only' s" and the unacceptance of the reality of loss. The "blame game" assumes it must be someone's fault...and in some cases, there is fault...even if it lies in the person who died. If someone had contributing factors, it's legitimate to hold them accountable, but the line of reason still moves up a rung on the impossible ladder. The questioning has a target." Since God is omniscient (all knowing), that means he knew." "Since he is omnipotent (all powerful), he could have done something about the situation." "Why did God let it happen?" "Why didn't he do something about it?" Now we have moved into the category of questioning God's integrity and goodwill.

The closer to the answer that we are demanding, or the closer to the truth we are really seeking is, "Why didn't God stop this from happening," or in other words, "Why didn't God interfere, or prevent my loved one from dying?" At some point we need to ask some self-examination questions and check our motives before we can honestly ask examining questions about God.

Why Am I Asking God Why?

In our hurt, we can find ourselves attached to the

inability and refusal to deal truthfully with anger. The ones who could bring us comfort and healing, we refuse to let comfort us if we are blaming them for the hurt and pain existing. Take notice of the husband-and-wife example. When couples find themselves at odds with one another, it can escalate into a major conflict to the point of casting hurtful verbiage towards each, because of a hurt-filled heart. At this juncture, the "blame game" is that "You hurt me and now I don't trust you or refuse to let you (also out of anger) bring any healing into my life because the way I see it, you are responsible for the hurt and pain being there!"

Now transpose this relationship issue over to God and humans. We refuse to let God comfort us since we blame him for the hurt. The biblical understanding is that God didn't cause the death, at least not actively. He didn't make it happen in a proactive way. God didn't cause the loss of my loved one, but since he could have prevented it, we wrongly assume it was God's inaction that caused it. This mindset more accurately is represented as "God should have prevented the death, and since he could have, he should have, so, then, God has a responsibility in the issue." With this (il)logic, what they are saying from their deduction is that God really had an obligation to stop my loved one from dying. Since he didn't respond to that obligation, I reason he is responsible for the death and consequently my hurt and pain. Continuing with that thought pattern, the mindset of as a victim sets in and we feel as if in some sort of cruel cosmic way that God has victimized us and the loved one, we lost. Further, since God hasn't revealed to us the reason for the death, so we can find some purpose or meaning to make acceptability of the reality more palatable, then we refuse to make up with him so that healing take place between us. We accept, and some embrace, the spiritual wedge that deepens and widens our faith factor. That's the examining study and observation that some do about God and the usual unfortunate effects that take place. Our bottom line - - "He should have done something!"

The First Question

Let's go down the road of self-examination and bare bones honesty about us and the truth of the matter; here goes the first question at the very high end of sounding extremely calloused, "What does God owe you?" That question doesn't appear with the indifferent shrug of a shoulder. It isn't asked with any condescension or derision. It is asked with intellectual and logical honesty. Again, "What does God owe you?" At the risk of stone throwing, what does God owe the person who died? To take this to its logical end-result, "What does God owe anyone? Can we be brutally honest without being brutal? These questions aren't meant to interrogate the truth out of someone living or hiding a lie. They are meant to stop a line of unreasonableness towards someone, from someone that has become unreasonable. Think about the implications of these questions and the impact of the answer. The blatantly obvious answer is that God owes no one anything! I repeat, He owes no one anything! He owes no justification for what he does or doesn't do. As put forth earlier, in God's omniscience (all knowing), he uses his wisdom and understanding on when, or not, to exercise his omnipotence (all power). Does God owe anyone taxes for the Earth that he created? Does God owe anyone money he never borrowed? Does God owe anyone thanks for any favors they think they did him? God is self-sufficient and existed just perfectly fine in the timeless past before he decided to create us. By the way, God can, does, and will get along without us. Remember, God is on Heaven's throne without a democracy.

"Well God owes me an explanation! For what; why? Why does God owe you an explanation for the death of your loved one? If that were true, he would owe everyone an explanation for everyone's loss; that's an awful lot of explaining to do. What justifies the arrogance of demanding answers to something we may not even understand? Of course, it is hurt and pain and the consequent irrational reasoning that comes from it. These self-examination questions leave repercussions that can bruise the ego.

The Second Question

Irrational Reasonings and Logical End Results

The second question that promotes self-examination goes like this, "If God should have stopped or prevented your loss, what makes you so special?" Why not obligate him to prevent everyone's loss? Why doesn't God just prevent everyone's accidents; even the ones that are brought about by carelessness. God should just stop all injustices; so what should God do to you if you're the one that is causing the injustice? God should stop all deaths. If so, what would we do with the aging population issues? If God should stop all tragedies, what constitutes a tragedy? Should we let the people take a vote on it? What should God do with those that plot or try to cause the tragedy? Perhaps try them for crimes against humanity? Should God intervene in all cases? What about all the people who want nothing to do with him; does it appear to be fair that God would intervene for everyone even when all are not his? Should God interfere with my freewill? Where does this line of (il) logic end? Is it okay if God lets me take a few drinks but somehow is obligated to stop me when I've had enough and am on the verge of becoming a danger to myself and others? What if someone is determined to lie; should God open their mouth and make the truth blurt out? Is it "right and truth" in every case? - - "Yes honey, you really do look fat in that dress!" Should God strike people with blindness that look at pornography? How should God stop things from happening?

So many people have their own judgments of the scope

of God's intervention. At some point, everyone would disagree as to who gets to make the decision of "who, what, where when why and how." Should God intervene in the affairs of men? Obviously that mindset exists in the mentality of anyone who says that God should or should have. What they are saying is that they now possess the infinite wisdom and discernment of knowing the answers and timing and ramifications of God's interventions. Logically, it seems that mankind can now entrust God's interventions with the rationale and logic out of someone's hurt and pain. In their defense they may add, "no, I'm only speaking for myself," but everyone who has experienced the loss of a loved one can make that claim. If we can admit God's infinite omniscience, and our lack thereof, then the judgments of God's interventions must remain exclusively with him. This is Faith. Be reminded though of this, we all have or will experience the loss of a loved one, just as God experienced with his son; both everyone who wants nothing to do with him and everyone who wants everything to do with him.

The Third Question

The third question -- Are we using our hurt or our loss as an excuse to walk away from God? There are those who have an ulterior motive or some hidden agenda that only exposes itself when an excuse of reason comes their way. The decision they make, or the path they take, seemingly is played out by the circumstances but the circumstances only serve as a cover for what they wanted to do anyway. Have you ever noticed that if some wrong is done to some people, then the offense they take seems to be blown way out of proportion? The secret reality is they may have been itching for a fight the whole time and the wrong becomes the offense of convenience to lash out, either to display behavior that otherwise wouldn't be tolerated or as an excuse to beat on the person who ostensibly caused their offence. We may not realize our actions and motives overtly.

Jeremiah 17:9, "The heart is deceitful above all things and beyond cure. Who can understand it?" Not many will admit their wrong actions and motives especially if it involves plotting. They become subdued beneath a thin veneer of unadmitted justification. We sear our conscience, as it were, with God and it kind of boils down to that some folks are itching for a fight with him. They are looking for some perceived hurt or injustice to come their way so they can use it to self-justify behavior that normally wouldn't be acceptable. Too often it is rebellion masquerading as hurt. Some people utilize the death of a loved one as the circumstance from which they can't recover, by blaming God. Since he is at fault, there can be no reconciliation. The next step is to give God the silent treatment and then to walk away from the relationship. Typically, the person ends up in a lifestyle that is contradictory to their previous faith and lifestyle. Since the lifestyle they had previously was connected to God, and the relationship they had with God now has a major disconnect, they move away from that connecting lifestyle into one that promotes a continued disconnect. Yet at the root of it wasn't the hurt and pain from the loss of a loved one, it was a rebellion that was waiting to happen. The death of a loved one, truth be told, wasn't the "straw that broke the camel's back;" too often it was an opportune moment, seized upon as an excuse to walk away from God. Yes, these are hard words! Hardcore words, for hardcore examinations, for hardcore situations. How bad is it that someone loses a loved one? How bad is it when someone besmirches the memory of a loved one by using their loss to justify rebelling against God? They can say they fell into or continued a wrong lifestyle because of their hurt and pain when really, they have been secretly longing to embrace that unacceptable lifestyle and now find refuge in a fig leaf of an excuse. Remember God's omniscience doesn't just know what you do or have done, he also knows why you do what you do or have done, and he also knows why you don't do what you don't do. Jeremiah 17:10, "I the Lord searches the heart and examines the mind."

Are we using your hurt and pain as an excuse to walk away from God, even blaming God? It is a legitimate question. It is not a catch-all reason by any means, yet it is a contributing factor for people who choose to disconnect their relationship with God. Perhaps in imposing this self-examining question, those affected people may come to their senses and turn away from their disconnecting attitudes and lifestyles.

Moral Credibility

Our fourth examining observation question, "If God didn't spare himself the tragedy and heartache of separation and loss through the death of a loved one, why is he obligated to spare us?" Remember that it was, and is proved, that The Father not only had a son but that the relationship was one in which The Father was well pleased. It wasn't like they were estranged or "on the outs" with one another. They were a close-knit family unit; there was tremendous value placed on the relationship by both. When the loss occurred, there was real hurt and pain for The Father. He didn't avoid the loss and the resultant heartache that any loving parent would experience. If someone is willing to experience something, especially to set an example or to make a sacrifice on behalf of others, they hold a high degree of moral expectations that some would follow suit." If I did it, you can do it too" is a popular refrain held by many who have achieved, accomplished, or endured. It usually is said as encouragement or motivation. To go to college, try for the promotion, get your chemo treatments, lose weight, learn to drive, recover from the breakup, learn a trade or new life skill, and the list goes on and on as it is said and applied to every demographic. Most results are motivation to achieve, accomplish and endure.

Some would split theological hairs and say that Jesus had to go to the cross and die. He was obligated to do so; The Father had no choice. Yes, in the sense that if someone was going to sacrifice their life for others, he was the only one who could go and achieve, accomplish and endure...and The Father knew this. If there was going to be a substitution for us that was acceptable, he was the only one who would be accepted, so therefore if it was going to happen, he would have to go. Yet Jesus said that he could call on The Father and stop the whole bloody mess. Matthew 26:53, "Do you think I cannot call on my Father and he will at once put at my disposal more than twelve legions of angels?"

On the other side of this argument, we see that God exercised his free will to let it all go down in the horrific fashion it did. Why? Because God the Father and the Son knew that this was the only real way to reconcile people back to them. Moving forward in the argument that Jesus had to go to the cross and die, the question is asked, for whom? The answer is, for you and for me. Isn't that unfair? Why should someone have to die for you or me? Remember, God didn't bring this on himself. It is not his fault that we are going through what we are going through. It's too bad and unfair that someone's son or child had to die for someone else. How would you feel if your child, no matter the age, had to give up their life for others?

There are those who lose loved ones because in their line of work, in their obligation and love to duty in serving their community, country or fellow humans; they make the ultimate sacrifice. When firefighters, policeman, and various rescue personnel rush into emergency situations and put their lives at risk, or lose them, in order to save others, we rightfully recognize the heroism. When soldiers trade their lives, when a citizen or relative steps out to protect, society remembers the loss. While the loss of these examples may give the mind something to understand, it doesn't give the heart any real medicine for its hurt. If someone dies saving or defending another so that they may live, it still doesn't take away much from the loss of the loved one who died. No matter how you cut it, I still suffered loss. The hurt and pain are still real. God does understand what it is to lose a loved one and he didn't spare himself from the separation. The loss of his child was unfair to him. Injustices and tragedy were the circumstances of his Son's death, yet The Father still chose to go through with this. Why? John 3:16, "For God so loved the world that he gave his one and only Son, that whoever believes in him shall not perish but have eternal life."

Faithfulness

Let's revisit something about this situation, God could have stopped this, but he chose not to because Jesus Christ had to go to the cross if God was to reconcile us. In a nutshell it goes like this: God was showing his faithfulness to us through the death of a loved one, His son.

God was revealing his character to the world and you, and I are included in the world. He was proving his commitment to people who didn't even know him or care about him. God was honoring his loyalty to people who hadn't been born yet. Remember, this death occurred over two thousand years ago." For God so loved the world," even when the world wasn't loving him. The Father set an unparallel example. He was willing to endure heartache and pain by losing a loved one in order to reach out to us. He didn't turn his back on us when he could have cut and run. God didn't use the death of a loved one as an excuse to get away from us; he used it as the means to draw closer to us. Now this brings us to a crossroads question that is also examining, "Since God showed his faithfulness to us through the death of a loved one, will we in turn show our faithfulness to him through the death of a loved one?"

Will we quit blaming God, and instead use it as a time to draw close to him and show our faithfulness in those times? Admitting our hurt and pain to someone who has "been there and done that" and who can speak into our soul's understanding and comfort. No matter the circumstances of the loss, knowing that The Father also had to bear losing a loved one comforts us. Accept the fact that we may not always understand why and decide to stay loyal and committed to God by walking in faith that he is who he says he is. God didn't call us to a walk of understanding; he called us to a walk of faith. Romans 1:17, Galatians 3:1, and Habakkuk 2:4, "The righteous shall live by faith."

Touch Me From Your Experience

God has all moral credibility by asking and expecting us to remain faithful to him, when he remained faithful to us, even when it cost him his child. Those who turn away from God when they lose a loved one are being unfaithful. Instead of running away from him, we should be running towards him. I believe there is a comfort and grace which becomes magnified when we pray that God would touch us from his experience. He has already been through this. God can bring us a word, a vision, a touch, a presence out of his limitless experience that he has felt which can overflow comfort into our sufferings. We don't always need our hurt resolved with answers; we just need to know that someone who has gone through what we are going through is there for us to lean on. You can be assured that God has gone through what you have, and you can call on him for hope and healing. Perhaps the first prayer that some may need to make would be along the lines of, "God, help me to show the same faithfulness to you over the death of my loved one as you have showed yourself faithful to me over the death of your loved one." The second prayer made as a follow up to this or any other situation we come to endure would be, "God, Touch me from your experience with this."

God understands. The next time the question arises, "Does God really understand death?" ...the loss of a loved one, the loss of my loved one, what I am going through... the answer must be, "Yes!"

Chapter 3

Does God Really Understand My Death?

At this point, the premise has been set... "Does God really understand what I'm going through?" Perhaps more specifically, "Has God experienced my experience, though maybe not my exact circumstances or my exact situation?" If he hasn't experienced specifics unique to me in practice, has he experienced it at least in principle? We are establishing the answer to be "Yes."

In the previous chapter, we dealt with a subject that is a heavy hitter...death! There is another perspective to death. Not only the loss of a loved one; what about the loss of oneself? What about my own death? Does God really understand my death? Does he understand separation? Our mortality? To be blunt, does God really understand my dying? Does he understand what we go through along the way? For some, it's not death that concerns them as much as the dying along the way. Sooner or later we all must face the loss of a loved one. just as sooner or later we all must face our own mortality. Some of us die unexpectedly, some die in our sleep. Some die after a long, arduous struggle with a disease. Holy scripture identifies the fact of our mortality.

Hebrews 9:27, "It is appointed to man once to die," and Ecclesiastes 3:2, "There is a time to die." There will come a point in time when we shall breathe our last. We can moderate our diets and avoid excess sugar, fat, cholesterol, and salt. We can exercise all the years that we have. We can avoid reckless lifestyles and behaviors; have jobs, careers, and family lives that are relatively stress-free. We can have good genetics in the area of family longevity. We can take supplements and get good health care for any afflictions that come our way. All these things contribute to a longer lifespan, yet our body will still age. Reflexes will slow down; muscular strength and speed will decrease; and one day the absolute inevitable shall happen -- We will die, whether we see it coming or not! In many cases death can be delayed or perhaps we should say, we can add time to our lives by the previously mentioned factors. While there is some truth to that, the great reality is what everyone knows -- There is a time to die.

Across the human divide are a wide range of responses to the dying. For some, death comes unexpectedly -- the sudden heart attack or brain aneurysm. How many try to avoid an untimely death though they are in some type of military war endeavor? Some are killed in various types of accidents, vehicular, boating, sports, or work. Accidents add to the column of the unexpected, that is, untimely deaths. Can you prepare for your untimely death? The spiritually minded may plead the case, "Well, if you have made peace with God, then who cares when you go? You are ready." Yes, you are ready to enter eternity, but you may not have been quite ready to depart now, especially being concerned with the loved ones you leave behind.

Some face the reality of their death with mocking and scorn. Others shrug it off not concerned with what comes after death. Some genuinely consider actionable consequences. "Who will take care of my kids? Or my spouse? The pets? What will happen to my family? The business?" These types generally do some form of preparation through living wills and have their Last Will and Testament prepared, especially for the sake of inheritance. Some go so far as to put money in a trust to pay for funeral and burial expenses. They make provision for the inevitable.

How can we face our own death? How do we face our own death? How can we help others face their own death? There are two typical aspects to death or dying -- imminent and eventual, the sooner or later views. Imminent means that the time of death is close at least in the sense that it will be soon by societal norms ... in a few days, a few hours or minutes. The hospice care is ending, the painkillers are the only treatment left, and the family members are called in. If you're conscious and aware, then you recognize it as close by, or imminent. To the contrary, eventual death implies that some time will pass by before the inevitable happens. You have years left, perhaps decades. No sense of urgency exists for the ones who think that they have time on their side. "Yes, it will happen someday. We've all got to go sometime. But it's not my time yet, so I don't care." For each of us the eventual (later) will become the inevitable (sooner). What then? Whenever the inevitable happens, in whatever form it does, we reach for comfort and hope in that last time frame. We may ask, "Can God relate to my dying? What experience does he have in this area?"

Knowing My Dying

Let's first establish some things. Remember the definition of Emmanuel, "God with us?" The bottom line was that God came to Earth among us as a human being. We'll look later at his humanity, but as God the Son became human, he not only was born as one of us, but he could also now die like one of us. This answers the question, "Can God die?" Not as fully God, which he is, but as fully human, which he was. Let's look at his own testimony in Matthew 20:17-19 where Jesus talks about his own death. Take notice of the who/what/when/where/how answers this passage gives about his death. Who would be involved? Himself, the chief priests, the teachers of the law and gentiles. What was it all about? For him to be handed over to his death. Where would it happen? In Jerusalem. When would it happen? During the week celebrating Passover, when they were about to be on their way. How would it happen? He would be mocked and flogged (whipped) and then crucified. Also, from John 12:32-33, "When I am lifted up" and "to show the kind of death he was going to die."

Jesus was foretelling, some would say predicting, the details of his own death. Some of us do happen to know what the cause of our death will be. The terminal. Those set to be executed. Very few of us know the details of the inevitable. How would you react if you knew the details of your own death before it happened? What if you knew the answers to the questions of your death? Jesus knew it was coming and how it was going to go down. He saw it as inevitable. He saw the later become sooner. And the sooner become imminent. In other words, his life, or what remained, became a countdown.

Can anyone imagine the mind games this would play on the average human? All of us live our lives in a countdown; we just typically don't know when the counting will end. How would you live out the remainder of time if you knew the hour of your death especially if it was imminent? What kind of frenzy would it place a person's mental state? What loose ends would you try to tie up? Who would you call? With whom would you spend your remaining time? What entertainments or indulgences would you take part in? What regrets would surface? What confessions would you make? Could you or would you come to accept it with any degree of calm or peaceful resignation? My death is a condition of life. For us to experience this life, we must accept the experience of death, or the process of dying, that goes along with it.

Acceptance can be easier for many if the situation has as its roots a long illness that hastens the process. When people are victimized by life's offerings through shortened life spans ... whether the cause was genetics, an illness, or an accident ... no one implies a calloused "Oh well, that's life," but some outlooks see death as welcome relief from the torment and suffering. When someone has what is termed "something wrong with them," those affected or observing their death may think that the dying finality, was welcomed.

Even though Jesus knew the timing and circumstances of his death; it had to be troubling to also know this while still in good health. How would most react to this? "There's nothing wrong with me and I'm still going to die. I haven't done anything deserving the death penalty, but I have one on me anyway." Jesus was not terminal, but his death was inevitable and imminent. Death for all of us is inevitable but inevitability takes on both sharpness and bluntness when factored with imminence. The terminal is faced with the inevitable sooner than later and Jesus was faced with the same principle. How did Jesus live out his life in response to the imminence of his death, and the dying along the way?

Matthew 20:17 reads, "He took the twelve disciples aside and said to them," and in John 12:7 he said that the perfume poured on him was for his burial. It's okay to inform others, to prepare them. When you get the news, it is appropriate to share that news with those with whom you are the closest. He informed those who mattered. He didn't broadcast his imminent death to everyone within earshot but was judicious about whom he told. It's okay to be open and honest. Usually, we need to talk about it and come to terms with it. Having conversations about the truth of this matter brings a preparatory mindset that readies itself for the inevitable moment. Hopefully this helps our souls be cushioned somewhat. The impact not as deleterious as it otherwise would have been. All because we communicated the truth.

If we knew how we were going to die, along with when, what anticipations or expectations would be in our minds? A smile and peacefulness? Fear and trembling preceding that moment, due not just to the timing of our death, but also the nature of leading up to death? When mixed with "how," becomes the great emotional multipliers in coming to terms with dying and death. If able to choose a long life with a so-called bad ending, or a short time left with a peaceful ending, the preferable is the long life with a peaceful ending. The dreaded is a short time left with a nasty ending. which is what Christ was facing.

The obvious issue in death is the physical body quits working. It shuts down, but what causes that to happen? In the preferable, it's because someone has lived a long life, the body has run its course and simply wears out and slowly grinds to a halt. In too many cases, the body has gone through some type of trauma, whether long-term, cancer, emphysema, etc., or something traumatic such as a car wreck, accidents, war injuries, etc. How many newspaper articles have we read, and how many people have we known, who came to their end because of the infliction of short-term physical trauma that led to their imminent death? No matter the spiritual rationalization of the death of Christ, the physical reality is that he lost his life due to physical trauma. Just look at some of the details: He was hit, he was flogged/whipped, had a crown of thorns shoved on his head and he was nailed to a cross through his hands and feet.

The Dying Along The Way

If there is another thing else that adds to God's understanding, it is that he knows what it is to be beaten up. Yes, Christ, being God, got beaten up. God got beaten up, badly! He experienced pain and hurt. Since God had a body, and that body was broken and bled, it can truthfully be said that God understands being wounded. Isaiah 53:5, "He was wounded for our transgressions." God basically suffocated and bled to death. His physical body was traumatized to the point of death. He died. God died. God personally died. He experienced it. His physical body ceased. It quit. This was the "dying along the way" that God experienced. Pretty much everyone was powerless to stop the inevitable. Who could stand up to the forces set in motion? In principle, as many are powerless to stop downward death spirals, so were the participants in this story. Some could only look on with disbelief and heartache. Mark 15:40-41 tells us his earthly mother, along with other women, looked on. Most of his disciples had deserted him and there were few at his death. How is it that others can't stand with you to see it through because of their own shortcomings? How terrible that some, in this case the Pharisees, gave consent and were happy that he was gone.

What is it like to die alone with no one who can help you, or no one will help you? Albeit on the battlefield, in a car wreck in a rural area, in a nursing home, or on the streets? God understands what it is to die a traumatic death with essentially no one to help him. With the cross as his deathbed, he understands what it is to not die in peace and comfort. As we look to Christ for our example, what example did he set in the face of the knowledge of his death with its imminence?

In John 13:1-17, Jesus washes his disciple's feet. Two revealing facts emerge. In verse 2, he mentions that the time had come for him to leave this world, acknowledging his impending death. In verse 15 he states, "I set you an example that you should do as I have done for you."

Living In My Dying

What positive examples can anyone emulate in the process of dying, particularly when death is irreversibly imminent? Christ set before us a model to be followed. The history informs us that he knew his time had come. He made an acknowledgment indicating acceptance of this reality. This isn't the way I want it, but it is what it is. He wasn't in denial or escapism mode. His mindset was to deal with his situation. He was spending time with those who were his followers. and even though his time was short, he refused to withdraw and be isolated. There he was, still sharing his time and imparting energy and counsel into the lives of the people who mattered to him. He didn't withhold himself, he kept giving. The witness is that he loved on them. Even when the end is imminent, we need to keep giving, sharing, experiencing, and loving.

What was he doing? Christ was living. He wasn't waiting around for death. He was living his life's purpose despite it. He didn't crawl in a corner; Jesus kept living! How, then, should we live our lives in response to the inevitable whether sooner or later? Keep living whatever life you have left! Keep on sharing your time and energy with those who matter to you. Keep on building relationships. Don't withdraw. Love on others. Express your love, not just in words but also in deeds. Jesus knew his time was short and he still set an example of love. He still had other people's best interests in mind.

So how should we live our lives, or what's left of it, in our time of dying? To the fullest extent possible, making the most of our situation, still creating memories, at least for others, and giving of ourselves unselfishly. This is the example of living in our dying that Christ revealed for us.

Praying In My Dying

Yet continuing to live life is not the only lesson to be learned from Christ's dealing with the inevitability and the tragic circumstances of his death. In John 17:1-5, we see Jesus prays for himself, in John 17:6-19 we find he prays for those closest to him, and in John 17:20-26 he is praying for others.

Let that be the lesson in and of it -- he kept praying and thus communicating with God. He didn't let the fact of his imminent death interfere with his prayer life. He didn't become despondent and quit talking to God. If anything, the inevitable advancing of his death prompted him to stay close to his Father. In John 17:1-5, where he is praying for himself, we see justification for considering yourself in your prayer life. There is no martyrdom to be had by never praying for yourself. It is not selfish to pray for yourself; it is important to include yourself in your prayer life. You should pray for your health, finances, marriage, character, and walk with God. The "what and why" of those prayers may become suspect because of motives but to ask God for help in any of these and other areas is not in and of itself wrong. Jesus prayed for himself. If we consider it was not wrong for him, and he is our prime example, it is not wrong for us. Praying exclusively for oneself is wrong. but never praying for yourself is even more wrong.

Jesus didn't just pray for himself, he also prayed for those closest to him. In the final remaining living in his time of dying, he interceded for others. He was still laying down his life daily, while his life was about to leave him. With time running out, most would become introverted. Yet he kept expressing love and consideration for others, recognizing others' needs and not just his own. His perspective of life wasn't self-centered, it was expansionist. His example says, "My prayers are not going to be only about me but will include those with me." The reality is, he wasn't just praying for his own needs, but had concern for others too.

Many of us, when faced with the end of our time here, become preoccupied within. Yet Christ's love, in what living time he had left, motivated his prayers for those close to him. He never stopped his intercessory prayers. John 17:20-26 reveals he prayed for others beyond his loved ones. How inclusive! Making intercession for others is an expression of love and unselfish giving. The example of living in our dying in John 17 is that we should not stop praying ... for ourselves, those closest to us and for others. When we do this, we are ratifying that we are going to live whatever life we have left.

Being Truthful In My Dying

Matthew 26:38, "My soul is overwhelmed with sorrow." In verse 39, "May this cup be taken from me" and in verses 42 and 44 we find the same. The Gospels of Mark and Luke bear similar witness. How did he live his life in response to the inevitable? He was truthful, and truthful in his prayer life. Why shouldn't we be truthful in our prayer life? If God already knows, why not just up and admit it, whatever "it" is? In response to the reality of what he was about to go through, Christ was being open and honest. It's okay to confess we're scared, if we are. It's okay to admit that we're sorrowful, that it's affecting our minds and that it can be overwhelming sometimes when the burden of reality comes crashing down. It's not disproportionate to feel overwhelmed when something that is overwhelming is happening. Let the tears flow and the heart beat faster. Get alone with God and have it out if you must. Confess your true feelings; he already knows. No one in their right mind wants to go through something painful and traumatic. Jesus understood that what he was about to endure was going to cost him something.

The most painful point of all was that he was "playing a losing hand." Some of us can see how our end will come and it's not pretty. We think, "This isn't really the way I want to go. "Emotional" resistance sets in. While we may resign ourselves to the moment of death, that specific point in the time of our separation, we still don't want any of the "pain of dying" along the way. Who does? No sane person. While we may "soldier up" or "man up," putting on the brave face at some point, let's please allow ourselves those moments of strength and courage when we break down before God, giving exposure and vulnerability to the one who sees and understands. Just let it happen. Christ was up front and center in saying that, on a personal note, he didn't want to go through the ordeal. As earlier stated, he said "May this cup be taken from me." It wasn't just a solitary prayer, but a repeated entreaty.

Being Faithful In My Dying

Matthew 26:39, "Not as I will, but as you will" and verse 42 reiterates, "May your will be done." How did Christ live out his last? He stayed faithful and obedient to God. How many would tragically fall apart into immorality or disbelief because they castigate the one who gives comfort and hope? Many of us fall in soul dirt, getting messed up instead of cleaned up on the inside. Jesus reaffirmed his allegiance and first love. This is his example, in essence saying "I didn't want to go out like this, but Father, if you don't change this course, so be it. If this is how I am to go out, proving who I am and who you are, then I shall. My preference is to avoid the process, but I won't, and I will do it faithfully. If I could have a choice, my choice would be avoidance, but there are more important things to consider than myself. My trust in you in that my living, and in my dying, would prove the more important things, even if I don't understand them. So let the life I have left be a witness that I shall be faithful to you no matter what. Not as I will, but as you will. I will entrust the proving of the more important things to you."

Making Provision In My Dying

How did Christ live out his life in response to the inevitable? Let's look at a few more verses. Luke 22:31-32, "That your faith may not fail." John 19:26-27, "Here is your son, here is your mother." These reveal that, faced with the prospect of his departure, Jesus needed and wanted to get a few things in order. Dying along the way becomes time to tidy up our affairs. Jesus, who had been a support structure for Peter, had legitimate concerns over the disciple's faith and he reassured him. If we were going to die, would we not rightfully be concerned about those for whom we have been a spiritual provider? Hopefully we could pray and leave them with a word of reaffirmation.

In Luke 22:36, Jesus gives instructions about preparing for, and provisions in, his absence. There is nothing unseemly about talking through the logistics of money, finances, healthcare, housing, religion, and such, in reference to the impact that someone's death is going to have. Don't put your head in the sand and ignore the consequences of anyone's death. Each death has some type of impact. How is the family going to make it financially? What benefits may be lost and what resources are available to make up for it? Will we still go to the same church? Do we have to move? What relationships are being affected? Time needs to be taken to prioritize and deal with death as a life-altering event, because lives will be changed as a result. Consider when he said, "Here is your son; here is your mother." With no welfare or social security system in that day, Jesus made family arrangements. John, the disciple, just had his household increased and Jesus' mother, Mary, gained a new son to take care of her needs. There is everything loving and caring about planning for our deaths. Most of us should be able to create wills, living wills, purchase life insurance, and make our wishes known to any capable surviving loved ones. Yet many of us put off partial, if not all, death planning. Doing so typically creates burdens, or sometimes more dramatically, outright conflict. Jesus set us examples of getting our house in order in anticipation of our deaths. This is not something morbid, rather a mature, responsible approach to life and death. If we really cared, we would prepare especially as we get closer to the inevitable in whatever way that plays out for us as individuals.

The Hope and Faith In My Dying

Let's look at another way that Jesus lived his life in response to the inevitable. In the Gospel of Luke 23:43, Jesus responds to the thief on the cross who requests that he remember him when Jesus comes into his kingdom, with, "I tell you the truth, today you will be with me in paradise." Also, in John 2:19-22, Jesus refers to his own resurrection from the dead when he says to the Pharisees, "Destroy this temple [referring to his own body] and I will raise it in three days." In John his death was not close by. In Luke, it was moments away. Yet in both instances, his response was with a future hope. He never forgot his destiny of being with God. To the thief on the cross, Jesus assures him that he will be in paradise with him. Declaring that he was moving on to something better. In John, we see that being in paradise wasn't enough; he was going to be reunited with his physical body. He would be resurrected. He lived whatever life he had left with a hope and faith that this life was not the end. What a compelling truth for us. That Jesus would face death knowing that it couldn't stop those who belong to God. We need to adopt the same mindset, attitude, and faith assurance. Jesus knew that his death was inevitable, but he also lived as if his afterlife and resurrection were also inevitable. So should we!

Forgiving In My Dying

Another example revealed in Luke 23:34, "Father, forgive them for they do not know what they are doing," is the act of making peace with those who are against us. The reality in his situation was that they didn't make peace with him. Yet he prayed for his enemies, extending peace and love toward them. Whether they accepted it or not, it was theirs. It wasn't a matter that Jesus had to clear his conscience, but maybe some of us do. What do we have to lose in our final moments anyway? Forgive those who have wronged us and pray for them. That is what grace is all about so give grace freely. Jesus gave grace freely all his life, and moves us by his final moments to, at the very least, release into eternity any wrongs, bad feelings and injustices before we are released into eternity with God. Forgive, make peace, and clear your conscience. and hopefully you'll do it now and not wait until the last to do so.

The Trust In My Dying

In Luke 23:46, we read the words, "Father; into your hands I commit my spirit." The last words of Jesus on Earth before his passing. What would be our last words if we had the time to think of them? Remember, the cross was Jesus' deathbed. The words on the cross were his deathbed confessions and instructions. His last words were words of trust. "Father, into your hands I commit my spirit." When we are about to breathe our last, words of trust that speak of what's next should pass our lips, and those words should be directed toward The One who is about to receive us. Can we confidently make this claim of faith? After everything we've been, and are going through; when it's all finally ending, will we close with a confession of faith? "Father, it's all up to you now. There's nothing I can do about what's going down and about to happen, but if there was ever a time when I am completely powerless and, in someone else's hands, it is now. And quite honestly and literally, it all comes down to this. At the very last, I ultimately am trusting in no one or nothing else. My spirit and my destiny I gave to you before death and keep on giving it to you at its door. Now I can let go and let God." Follow his example.

I Haven't Experienced This Before

What is it about death that concerns us so much? It's because we've never experienced it. When we experience things, we become familiar with them. Death (separation) is permanent in our minds, even though in some manner it's not permanent. We are eternal beings in that we will always exist. It's just a matter of where and how. Will we exist eternally with God, or will we exist eternally without God which is defined as "the second death." Will we be in his hands or not?

If we've never experienced something, and it's a big event or of great importance like death, then most normal reactions would be nervousness, trepidation, and anxiousness. Since death is separation, the concern about death is separation anxiety. "I've never experienced this separation, and it concerns me." When Christ said on the cross in Mark 15:34, "My God, my God, why have you forsaken me?" the traditional and accepted view is that the sins of the world had come upon Jesus, and he felt removed from the Father because of it. While that is primarily the theological truth, I also believe that a contributing factor was that Jesus was experiencing separation anxiety, the death-separation that he was about to undergo. Be reminded, God himself up to this point had never experienced death on a personal level and it was about to happen. I don't believe it was fear, but more of a question of "What is this going to feel like? How is this going to process?" In his human form, Christ could feel the limitations imposed. He may have known what was coming but had never experienced it. Scripture informs by him saying "Into your hands I commit my spirit" that any separation anxiety soon was outweighed by his faith and trust in God's plan.

When we are faced with separation anxiety about the experience of death because we haven't gone through it before, let us be comforted in the truth that God has gone through it and understands. How should we face our own death and help others to face theirs? By following the examples that Christ lived in his dying.

How To Live In My Dying

Let's recap the examples of how Christ lived his life in the face of dying, as the proof has been unfolded that God really does understand my own death since he died himself. Do I yet understand how to live in my dying? While this list is in no way exhaustive, it gives us quite a bit to go on.

Here's the summation -- Don't let mind games and lies affect you. Take ownership of the situation at least as far as the truth of the matter is concerned. Face the truth of inevitability. Sooner or later death comes knocking at the door. Later always becomes sooner at some point. We may delay it, but we cannot prevent it. Inform others, talk about it. Don't bury your head in the sand and try to be a lone hero. Others have a right to know and to also get prepared. Keep living, sharing and loving. Keep living the life you have left! Don't crawl up in a corner and act like it's all over. When it's over, then it's over, and not any sooner. Pray and communicate to God; involve him. He's already been through the valley of the shadow of death, and he can certainly speak to your spirit, words and feelings of experience. Be honest and open about all the realities. The physical decline, the emotional burden, and the spiritual struggles. Stay faithful to God to hear him say "Well done, thou good and faithful servant" (Matthew 25:21). He's been faithful to us, now is the chance to prove ourselves faithful to him. Get things in order. Let everything be done decently and in order including the handling and transfer of our affairs after we're gone. Remember your destiny and hope. For the non-Christian, this life is the best it ever gets; but for the Christian, this is the worst it ever gets. Make peace with others and your soul. Release forgiveness. Why not also leave these types of things behind? Trust God. "Into thy hands..." (Luke 23:46). Try to make these your last words of confession, moving from faith to faith.

This chapter was written to answer the question "Does God really understand my own death and the dying along the way?" The response is "yes", and he also set examples of how to live in our dying.

Chapter 4

Does God Really Understand My Temptation And Inner Conflict?

We are tempted by things that we don't want to do, or at least say we don't want to do. Situations or actions that we wish to avoid or the activities in which we try not to engage. How many people are tempted by negative comments they want to make, but discern that they should refrain? We resist doing or saying things for many reasons but, in general, we resist because we realize the negative consequences such as penalties of some nature, perhaps a guilty conscience, or maybe disapproval by others. Temptation is an appeal to satisfy some inner urge. When we resist temptation, it usually leads to some degree of inner conflict. The part of me which is resisting the part of me which wants to give in. The urge is like forward momentum; the more it is entertained and thought about, the more the forward momentum increases creating a greater inner conflict when I apply resistance. As always, the urge is toward the desire that has the most powerful appeal. only to be resisted by the reality of consequences. We register thousands of temptations as we walk this life; some we give in to immediately, others we don't. However, there is no inner conflict if there is no resistance. It's only when we resist that we find ourselves against ourselves. That's why it's called "inner" conflict."

God Suffered

When we think of God being perfect, sometimes we have this picture of someone who is "cool, calm, and collected," as the saying goes, sitting on his throne in Heaven with no problems or cares at all. Wistfully giving commands for angel dust to be sprinkled on the clouds. Returning to the earlier reality that God himself lived as a human, as one of us, Hebrews 2:18 reads, "Because he himself suffered when he was tempted, he is able to help those who are being tempted." That one scripture reveals that God experienced temptation; he can help us because of his experiences ... and he suffered in his temptations.

The Pain Of Resistance

The especially revealing issue is that he suffered in his temptation. What was the suffering? It was the "pain of resistance." He struggled so much in his inner conflict that it led to actual pain. This seems to be the crux of the temptation/inner conflict issue -- We resist a temptation and the more we resist something we simultaneously desire, the greater the inner conflict. The longer the inner conflict goes on, or the greater the intensity level, the more we must resist which brings on progressive levels of discomfort until we are in the realm of the "pain of resistance".

Hebrews 2:17, "For this reason he had to be made like his brothers, in every way, in order that he become a merciful and faithful high priest in service to God, and that he might make atonement for the sins of the people." This is a scripture proving that God in Christ became human; "made like his brothers." However, the "in every way" part speaks to our point. For Christ to be subject to temptation, just like us, he would also have had the possibility of failure. What would be the big deal to give in to temptation if there were no consequences? Would it even be temptation? God, especially as a human, made like us in every way, would now be faced with the real possibility of failure by giving in to whatever desires, however strong. In his own humanity, undergoing what we go through in temptation and inner conflict, and experiencing the pain of resistance, he would now be able to intimately identify with our struggles. Hebrews 4:15 reads, "For we do not have a high priest who is unable to sympathize with our weaknesses, but we have one who has been tempted in every way, just as we are – yet was without sin."

There we have it -- Our God has experienced what we have gone through, he can and does relate to us. But it doesn't end with that; it goes on to state in Hebrews 4:16 "Let us then approach the throne of grace with confidence, so that we may receive mercy and grace to help us in our time of need." God has gone through everything we have gone through, either in practice or in principle, made like us in every way (Hebrews 2:17) and tempted like us in every way (Hebrews 4:15). Armed with that knowledge, we can be assured that he understands. When we are in our time of need, faced with inner conflict, needing help to overcome and forgiveness, we can find it in the one who is able to empathize (identify) with our weakness.

I John 2:16, "For all that is in the world, the lust of the flesh, and the lust of the eyes, and the pride of life, is not of the Father, but is of the world." All temptation falls under one of those three categories. The things we are tempted by. The resistance we have, the sins we have, all come under those three; that is, "all that is in the world." Jesus Christ had three great temptation episodes in his life and ministry. The first was in the wilderness, the second was in the Garden of Gethsemane, the last upon the cross.

Being Tempted By Need

After Jesus' water baptism by John, Matthew 4:1-11 informs us of Jesus being led into the desert to be tempted by the devil. The first intriguing point is that he was led. This was on purpose, for a testing. The tempter wasn't some fly-by-night tempter-in-training; it was the "father of lies" himself, the deceiver, the devil. One-on-one!! Verse 2 states, "Jesus fasted for forty days and nights, and then he was hungry." Who wouldn't be hungry after one day? So that's where he was tempted, in his hunger. The tempter was going after the lust of the flesh. In verse 3 the tempter says, "If you are the Son of God, tell these stones to become bread." "If," the biggest little word in our vocabulary is "if." By using that word in this manner, it was meant to be a challenge. The devil challenges Jesus with food to satisfy the craving of his hunger. Look at the circumstance -- He had gone without eating for forty days and nights. Quite some time by any standard. You can be challenged to sin not just by your cravings but also by your "needs." In your need, you can be tempted to do the wrong thing. His life situation, at that moment, was that he was in the desert, alone, hungry, and had just come off some spiritual high points. He was in a dry place in his life, no one around for support; he was in physical need and spiritually he was now in a valley or a low spot. His baptism had just happened, his ministry was taking off, and now this! No one's ever on the mountaintop forever. We all go through dry seasons. We all have times in our lives when we're vulnerable and alone. The devil will always tempt you at your weakest point.

Adam and Eve were also tempted with food. The one thing that God forbade, fruit of the forbidden tree, seemed to be the one thing they wanted the most. Because it had appeal, it would give them something they wanted but at what cost? With what "forbidden fruit" are we being tempted? At what cost to give in? Remember, you can be tempted to do the wrong things even to meet your "needs." Sin is like water and electricity; it follows the path of least resistance. Wherever there is a weak spot in your life, that's where the greatest potential for a spiritual leak is found. Some temptations (pressures) are greater than others, at least perhaps for a season in your life. Those temptations will require greater degrees of resistance, not the path of least resistance.

We have different levels and areas of temptation, desires, especially considering our different circumstances and stages of life. Young people may have more issues with some desires than when they get older. At any given point in life, some of us may have more of an urge to satisfy greed, revenge, or hate. Today it's me; tomorrow it's you. We each have weak areas we need to be cognizant of and properly safeguard against. What may be serious temptation for one person, another has no issues dealing with, and the converse is true. One constantly gives in to lying while another succumbs to lust. Someone else struggles with drugs yet another with sins of the tongue.

Most people have some urge to spend money unwisely or unnecessarily. Yet for some demographics, the urges are different. Let's look at genders. How many purses or pairs of shoes does any one woman really need? Then again, how many guns or fishing tackle boxes does any one man need? How many times do we have to buy new furniture or change the color schemes of the rooms in our homes? Do we really need the biggest surround sound for viewing our sports games? Control of our budgets has gotten many a household in trouble for giving in to temptations. How many of us have gotten into even more trouble by not resisting the urge to say something, especially in an untimely moment?

The #1 American Temptation

I think the single most common temptation Americans have, is the eating temptation. Americans are constantly encouraged to eat and at the same time are encouraged to lose weight. Eateries in every corner of the country offer food at reasonable prices, with snack foods of all kinds, and commercials all over the place tempt citizens with mouth-watering and belly-lusting desire. There are commercials all over the place wanting you to purchase their products to exercise, to lose the weight, with all the latest fads, gadgets, and crazes to have at home or at fitness centers.

How many New Year's resolutions or "first thing Monday morning" and "right after the holiday" commitments to lose weight and get in shape, are thrown under the bus when the resistance level involves saying no to our favorite dishes, engaging in social food activities, or reaching for our emotional comfort food when we're upset? There is a simple way to lose weight; consume fewer calories than you take in! But simple doesn't always equate, to easy. We resist for a season, maybe minutes in some cases, or months in others. Eventually the desire becomes stronger, especially the longer the denial. Most of us want an easy fix. I wish I could win a "lose fat and get in shape overnight" lottery, but life is what it is, and we must resist the urge to overindulge if we want to get to a reasonable target weight for ourselves.

In Matthew 4:5-6, the tempter goes after Christ in the category of "the pride of life" when he takes him to the holy city (Jerusalem), has him stand on the highest point of the temple, and asks, "If you are the Son of God, throw yourself down. For it is written -- He will command his angels concerning you, and they will lift you up in their hands, so that you will not strike your foot against a stone." The word "if" was used again. This time to bring doubt as to his nature, and to God's care for him.

In similar fashion this is what the devil used on Adam and Eve in the garden in Genesis 3:1-5 when he brought doubt into their relationship with God. Adam and Eve were caught up with the pride of life in the deceit that they could become like God. They believed a lie. It's been said that people won't die for a lie, but they will if they believe the lie is the truth especially when they are driven by the pride of life. "What's in it for me?" Back to the holy city, Jesus was being tempted to prove who he was with the pride of life -- "Go ahead, throw yourself down, and let's see a miracle" is what the devil was tempting. Yet in this event, Jesus wasn't just faced with ordinary circumstances. He was already hungry, had been in the desert, and now was up against the "father of lies".

What Can I Get Away With?

There are notable points in Matthew 4:5 -- Jesus was in the Holy city, standing on the temple, at its highest point. This represents a serious religious experience. A higher spiritual reality than anyone else could imagine. The temptation was in taking Jesus to the most significant holy spiritual place of their day, dare him to jump and prove who he was by the angels' keeping him from being killed. This was more than just "show us who you are;" this was "show us what you can get away with!" That is what is putting God to the test. "Thou shalt not tempt the Lord thy God (Matthew 4:7). How many people take things to the extreme to try to get away with something? Criminal activity is the epitome of trying to get away with something. In this case, God didn't ask Christ to take a leap of blind faith on his behalf, so for Christ to do it as the devil's suggested would be to tempt the grace of God. A foolish thing indeed. This would perhaps be a literal example of the scripture "Pride goeth before a fall," to paraphrase Proverbs 16:18.

Adam and Eve were faced with the same temptation, the pride of life, the promise that they would become like God. "Go ahead and eat, look at what you can get away with. Your eyes will be opened. There's a new reality awaiting you, a higher spirituality, and a better religious experience. You can be like God. You should be like God." Jesus was taken to the highest point of the holy city's temple. He too tempted to see what he could get away with and to show everyone who he was, the son of God. Both temptations hitting at their "pride-spots."

These accounts also have in common that they include examples of lust of the eyes -- Matthew 4:8, when the devil takes Jesus to a very high mountain and shows him all the kingdoms of the world, and Genesis 3:6, when Eve sees that the fruit of the tree was good for food and pleasing to the eye. Adam and Eve believed a lie because they thought they would get something out of it even when they knew that God had forbade it for their own good. Eve caught a vision ("lust of the eyes") of the wrong thing. The devil wanted Jesus to catch a vision of all the splendor of all the kingdoms of the world saying he could have it all if he would do only one thing, bow down and worship him (Matthew 4:9). The "pride of life" and "lust of the eyes" make us think and believe unrealistic things about ourselves and our relationship to God.

Christ was tempted in each category, in every way, as we are. He suffered through temptation. How many of us have been led by God through that kind of wilderness experience? All of us go through "dry" times in our lives. When those seasons or events come, how do we fare?

My Divided Self

How do you know what you're made of until you go through some hard times? No one wants to go through bad times, or find themselves in hard places, or in extremely difficult circumstances. However, when we do, that's when "the rubber meets the road;" where character, maturity, and even commitment is involved. Many marriage vows are made with the words "in sickness and health, for richer or poorer, for better or worse." What happens when sickness, poorer, and worse come at us? What happens when the moment of confrontation comes into my soul that divides me? What happens when the part of me which wants to give in to desire and temptation, and the part of me which knows better, comes into conflict? "A house divided cannot stand" and yet, even within myself, I'm divided. When I come up against something I know I shouldn't do or say - - there's a popular saying along the lines of "That which doesn't kill me makes me stronger." However, if I resist even to death, what kind of strength did I exhibit? "Resistance is futile," to what end is it futile? To my own end? If I resisted to my own end, was it futile or was I showing my strength?

How much resistance do we engage in? How much of a fight do we put up? How far do we take it? How long do we go? Most would agree that it depends on what is at stake. What are the consequences or the fallout? What is the exact situation? A person's inner strength is typically measured by what they have gone through, endured, and overcome. Many people think more of themselves than they should. They have an inner boast that comes through self-deceit, conceit, and an over-reliance on self. When troubles come their way, they fall apart at even little provocations. How strong are we when we lose a job, and we want to "throw in the towel" on life? When the marriage hits some rocky roads, some take a walk because it's easier to give up than to fight for what they vowed. They don't resist.

Many Christians think that because they have material happiness, they are secure and mature when the reality is that if they were being persecuted like their Christian siblings in some other countries, they would be the first to quit and denounce their faith. One group are martyrs; the other group are quitters. How many people have stumbled and then wanted to toss their lives out the window? Please remember this -- Just because you stumble doesn't mean you should throw yourself down the steps! Everyone makes mistakes and must pick up the pieces and move on in God's grace and forgiveness. From the dieter who eats a handful of cashews and then rationalizes that they can't resist, so they end up eating the whole can to the flirt who keeps flirting until they are engaged in a full-blown affair.

Whatever the degree of temptation, we must apply a greater degree of resistance. Many times, it will cost you something, usually time and energy. The longer the duration of some temptations, or the desire to fulfill it, the harder the resistance becomes until eventually it develops into pain. The longer the duration or intensity level of resistance, the greater the likelihood you will experience the #1 taboo word in the western church today and that is "suffering."

What is your tolerance level for pain or suffering? How much inner conflict in resisting temptation can we endure? This conflict isn't about a fist fight. This is a conflict that is internal and deeply spiritual, so how far do we take it? Do we take it to the point of suffering? Do we experience the pain of resistance? No one wants to suffer. but to resist some desires and deny ourselves, we may have to.

Being Faced With The "No"

No child ever wants to be told "no." Everyone has

witnessed a child's temper tantrums and displays of anger and tears when they are told "no" about certain things. Many times, it's because they don't understand, at least not yet. At other times, it's simply because they don't want to be denied, so you may need to get hearing protection on as the scream fest begins, especially in the middle of a crowded shopping area. Do we adults react any differently, at least emotionally, inside? The screaming is going on inside me. No one likes being told "no" especially when it's something that we really want. How dare anyone deny me!

Adam and Eve were faced with the "no." At some point, they came to want the "no." In their case, this was the forbidden fruit. We're all like that. We want what we can't, or shouldn't, have. It's almost as if there's an automatic attraction to what we can't have. The forbidden thing. The "no." "I want the no." "I want the no-thing." "Me, myself and I" are in a struggle within. Most struggles are ours, of course; it wouldn't be a struggle if it didn't involve you. We can't resist for each other. I can only resist for myself.

We all, at one time or another, find a way to "self-justify" our giving in to our resistance to temptation. Knowing we want to give up and give in, we rationalize why we should or must. For example - - Even though married, I'm in love with someone else, so the "I'm in love with someone else" excuse self-justifies the adultery and betrayal of my vows. If I tell the truth, I'll get into trouble so the "avoid getting into trouble" excuse self-justifies lying. We find ourselves screaming and belittling someone because we had to "get something off our chest," so we show malice and a lack of self-control. The "I just tell it like it is" and "get it off my chest" excuse is used to self-justify immaturity and bad behavior. Can we resist doing wrong things or do we purposely deceive ourselves and believe our own lies in order to satisfy sinful behavior, actions and attitudes? Another way we justify giving in to temptation is to resist for a little while and then fold, still feeling good about ourselves by rationalizing, "Well, I tried for a little while. I gave it a shot. After all, no one goes to the bitter end." We placate our consciences with some resisting. "It took longer than normal. I didn't just lie down and give up. Give me some credit!"

Knowing that you will do the inevitable on purpose, but delaying it so you can soothe your conscience, is really searing your conscience. Again, did we get to the "pain of resistance? I want the "no", and the want is being denied. How far do I take it? What are the repercussions, consequences, or fallout from giving in? What are the rewards, personal growth, and self-respect that are gained from not giving in? How important are those? What does this mean to my God, family, and future? The temptations lead to resistance; the resistance leads to pain; the pain leads to suffering. There are temptations that lead to suffering. Are we prepared for this? Are we aware of our weak spots?

Are we ready to deny self? Are we ready to say "no" to the "no thing?"

An Example Of The Pain Of Resistance

I think one of the greatest struggles ever recorded about inner conflict is detailed in three different Gospels. Matthew 26:36-46, Mark 14:34-39, and Luke 22:39-46 give accounts of the inner conflict and turmoil of what Jesus' thought, felt and struggled with in the Garden of Gethsemane. While we will look at these examples, the bottom line of his struggle was that he knew the horrors of what was before him in the ordeal of mock trial, beatings, taunts, and mainly his death by crucifixion, with his personal repulsion at the upcoming experience. All of us have become physically tense, upset, and even distraught over anxiety-producing news, or experiences that we undergo. When we are on the verge of going in for that much anticipated job interview, most of us have some physical response. Perhaps it's dry mouth, clammy hands, eye twitches, or quick, shallow breathing? What kind of events or news brings on our bodies' nervousness? What physical reactions do people have to different events? Some get headaches while waiting for things to unfold or events to pass. The body responds to different stresses in different ways for different people. Some get anxiety attacks; others' responses may include higher blood pressure or ulcers. The news of a death in the family, a tragic report from the doctor, or the unknown result of a situation with life-altering outcomes, bring about physical responses in each of us, no matter how calm we try to be.

We cry, we get angry, we become sullen and yet the admittance is that each of us has physical results from the emotions within. Our obvious and natural inclination is to resist the unpleasant. No one wants to go through dark hours. The body manifests the inner turmoil that is going on. It will especially expose that turmoil when there is emotional distress that involves the resistance of our will. This inner conflict, especially over temptation, is what Jesus went through in the Garden of Gethsemane.

In Matthew 26:37-38, Jesus "began to be sorrowful and troubled. Then he said to them, 'My soul is overwhelmed with sorrow to the point of death. Stay here and keep watch with me.'" There it is right up front and center -- God was admitting that he had inner conflict, even to the point of death. His problem was so big that it seemed bigger than he. That is mind-boggling that God was going through such a hard time, emotionally, that he would phrase it that this issue would take him to his limit. How much heartache can a person take before their breaking point? But he was the word of God made flesh, as a human being. Remember, in Hebrews 2:17, the scripture states, "For this reason he had to be made like his brothers, in every way." God came into the world as one of us to suffer temptation and to go through the most serious inner conflicts imaginable so that we might appreciate that we have a God who understands these experiences in the most incredible and intimate way possible. All he asked was that those who were closest to him would be there for him while he endured. Matthew 26 continues in verse 39, "Going a little farther, he fell with his face to the ground and prayed, 'My Father, if it is possible, may this cup be taken from me. Yet not as I will, but as you will.'"

He went a little farther away from them because he knew that this was one-on-one between, he and the Father. His request was for the disciples to be close by. Somewhat alone, he falls with his face to the ground, a position of humility, and he prays. This is the example we should all emulate. When something drastic is going on in our lives, we must pick up the pace and intensity of spiritual questing. "Desperate times call for desperate measures." We can't just think about praying, we must get down to the action of prayer. Now he calls out to Father and makes his request known, "I do not want to go through with this! Might this 'cup' be taken from me?" When we are terribly upset over any situation, it is not wrong to pray for God to take us out of it, to make the situation better, or to help us avoid worse. It is not wrong for us to want things to not be wrong! The issue is that we don't do wrong when things are wrong or going wrong. It's okay to want to not suffer, to not endure more, or to not hurt. It's okay to pray to God about it. The difference is what Jesus prays, along with the "Please make this go away" type of petition. He also prays, "Yet not as I will, but as you will." In his spiritual abhorrence there is also spiritual concession. At least the "mustard seed" beginnings of it. On one hand he is praying for a reprieve from an upcoming ordeal; on the other hand, he has recognized God's sovereignty and his personal resignation to his destiny. However, there was no doubt to the toll this was taking on his emotions, health, and body.

These three gospels reveal that as Jesus got up from his first entreaty to the Father, he returned to his disciples and found them sleeping. On top of his own inner struggle, with his darkest hour about to come upon him, he experiences the disappointment that those closest to him were not "keeping watch" with him. Not even for one hour. In other words, staying awake, being prayer partners of some sort, and perhaps commiserating at some level with his situation. He wanted reaffirmation that he wasn't alone. A revealing thing is spoken by Jesus when he says, "The spirit is willing, but the flesh is weak." Commonly, we believe that refers to the fact that the disciples were sleeping instead of praying. However, I also believe he was hinting at his own temptation and inner conflict. If he had also gone to sleep, is it possible that he wouldn't have come to terms with the decision he had to make because he wouldn't have been awake to pray and receive the strength the ministering angel gave him? How much he must have needed that strength Luke 22:44

reads, "And being in anguish, he prayed more earnestly, and his sweat was like drops of blood falling to the ground."

How many of us have ever resisted anything, and that includes resisting ourselves to the point of pain? The physical toll was intermixed with the emotional and spiritual. It is recorded that we humans can undergo such stress that blood can come out of our pores. The temptation and inner conflict were that, on a personal level; Jesus didn't want to go through with what was about to happen to him and, quite honestly, he didn't have to do this for his own sake. In Matthew 26:53, Jesus asks," Do you think that I cannot call on my Father, and he will at once put at my disposal more than twelve legions of angels?" A telling piece of information that going to the cross wasn't for his benefit; it was for ours! He knew the impact of his decision would be unbridled horror for him, but to not go would leave a spiritual distance between us and God that the Father wanted removed. This was the will of the Father. Jesus knew it was coming, he had prophesied it a few times and so had previous scripture. In our times of struggle and inner conflict, do we submit ourselves to do the right thing in the eyes of God, even if it involves suffering? What can be the turning point? It is the moment we decide that no matter what, we are going to do the will of God, even if it kills us!

Truthful Confession

No matter the anguish of our soul, no matter whether others are standing alert interceding with us or not, no matter our personal desires and prayers for this crisis moment to pass – in times of distress, what truth about ourselves will we confess? Jesus admits his sorrow, his anguish, his request that he could avoid what was about to happen. He admits that deep down in his heart he was willing to obey ("the spirit is willing") but every other part of him was screaming to be cut loose ("the flesh is weak"). It's that kind of confession (truthfulness) and resolve ("your will be done") that will bring about God's the grace to endure and overcome the pain of resistance.

The Bible is full of accounts of temptation, but we don't technically need the Bible to give us those examples. We need only to look at the lives of everyone we know, and that includes ourselves. Temptation is all around us, enticing, alluring, and standing at the door of our hearts. When it comes our way, we would do well to be reminded to speak to the source of the temptation. Get to the root cause. What are we engaged in, with what relationships and personal desires must we deal with and perhaps eliminate or at least restrict? In doing an honest evaluation, what resistance have we offered up against temptation?

Spiritual Points Made

Understand the implications or consequences of giving in to, or overcoming, bad desires. Pray the truth of how you feel about it at your personal level. Speak the truth of God's word against it. Don't justify giving in or believing a lie on why you should continue in the path of sin. Don't appease your conscience by resisting for a while, knowing you'll purposely give in at some point. Be resolved that more than anything, this is a spiritual confrontation that may involve the pain of resistance; that it might get harder and harder. Know that, at some point, you may cross the line into suffering. Keep resisting until that temptation no longer offers an appeal or opportunity as enticement. Remember, the answer to the question "Does God really understand my temptations and inner conflicts?" is "yes." Because of that, he is quick to answer prayer with empathy, grace, and compassion.

Chapter 5

Does God Really Understand Life's Odds 'N' Ends?

Church Splits

Does God really understand church splits? Historically, the spiritual reference of the church has meant its people under the banner of Christianity and the name of Christ. When we say we're going to church, we are simultaneously indicating a building and those who meet in it. Our reference is dually a geographical location and people who share our beliefs. Primarily, though, the church is the body of believers, locally or globally. When one hears of a church split, it's not the building that gets divided, it's the people who are dividing. Typically, it's a local church, but sometimes it is a whole denomination and its followers who are splitting, or dividing, over issues that they can't or won't reconcile. Church leaders are usually at the forefront of these divisions. Sometimes, a parting of company must be made for what is perceived as essential differences and no one holds hostilities. At other times, the division occurs because leaders rise to cause dissension and unrest for ignoble motives, and that's tragic. This section is written for all those who have undergone a church split, especially those in leadership. How to find recovery afterward? and what does God know or understand of a church split?

Based On A True Story

Once upon a time, long, long ago, a kingdom was established in Heaven. The Lord God Almighty sat on the throne and there was peace throughout the universe. The whole angelic body of believers, the heavenly church, worshipped and served together in this kingdom. Then one day, a worship leader named Lucifer was found to have pride (sin) in his heart. He wasn't satisfied to have a major part; he wanted to dethrone the king and he rose into battle. The worship leader had a powerful influence on one-third of the congregation, and he led them into open conflict against the king's court. The rest of the king's court held strong for their allegiance to the Lord God Almighty. All the angels who rose with Lucifer were cast out, and lost their membership, because they no longer wanted the Lord as their pastor. Then Lucifer and the congregation he stole, off the Pastor-Father-God, set up shop in one of the neighborhoods that the Pastor-Father-God had as his campus. It was Earth. Not content to have lost his challenge to take over the heavenly church, Lucifer decided to wreak havoc on the unsuspecting souls who populated the outreach campus. He cast aspersions and lies on all who would listen and defamed the name of the Pastor-Father-God so that few would become part of God's earthly campus congregation. Nonetheless, the Pastor-Father-God would continue his outreach with love anyway.

Admittedly, I simplified the story with language embellishments, but the reality remains intact -- God had a church split through a rebellious leader, within his own congregation, who wasn't content to just do his damage in-house, so to speak, but went out and continuously went against everything and anything that God was doing in the local community. Lucifer also pitted himself against all those who aligned with the "Pastor Father God." This process is analogous to many of today's church splits. Someone wants to be "top dog," or they have unreconciled matters with their church and its leadership. Instead of seeking understanding and resolution, they promote rebellion typically because they have pride issues and seek satisfaction, even at the expense of division. Think of all the hurt and pain that comes with losing one-third of your people, all due to "one bad apple" furthering a selfish agenda. The cruel part is that some can't just go quietly;

they seem obsessed with making all the noise they can muster, drawing attention to their dissension.

This hurts potential new converts and mature followers. It is a heartbreaking and sad commentary on character. Friendships are lost and relationships are gone. All the good that was done, or could have been kept going, has a stain on it. This had to be a grieving affair for the "Pastor Father God" who fellowshipped with all the angels who rebelled. The investment of himself into who they were, only now to observe the dysfunction that they followed, embraced and promoted. Ministries had resources taken from them; the "Pastor Father God" had his reputation maligned and that same character, who began the mess, is still trolling around, instigating trouble and crises.

How many church leaders and pastors can relate to what happened to God? It happened to him before it happened to you. A realistic reading of scripture reveals that God really does understand church splits.

Socializing And Dialoguing

Does God know what it is to go and hang out...unwind... "kick your shoes off?" We know through scripture that he had his retreat times with his disciples; he went further than that. In John 2:2, he is found at the wedding in Canaan, as a guest of someone's celebration. In Luke 4:38, Jesus left the synagogue and went to the home of Simon. In Luke

7:36, he attended an event with other guests at Simon the Pharisee's home and reclined at the table, just "chillin.'" He said to Zacchaeus in Luke 19:5, "Today I must stay at your house." He visited the home of siblings Mary, Martha, and Lazarus. The disciple and later apostle Peter had Jesus to his residence. Jesus socialized with a Samaritan woman when such a thing was frowned upon (John 4:27). Luke 5:29-30, "Then Levi held a great banquet for Jesus at his house (Jesus understands what it is to be the guest of honor) and a large crowd of tax collectors and others were eating with them." Because of certain associations and fraternizing with the so-called "riff-raff," Jesus was accused of being a friend of sinners, drunkards, and gluttons, all because he was willing to socialize and converse with them. He ate and drank, talked, and shared; listened and communicated. Yet he wasn't influenced by them; they were being influenced by him. He had fellowship with his community and intermingled with the greater circle of his associates, crossing rules of cultural engagement. People were and are important to Christ. God, in the form of man, socialized and dialogued at events small and large, public and private, to individuals and to the crowds.

Confrontation

Few people like confrontation but we can't always avoid things that are unpleasant and discomforting. Sometimes we must confront and hope it will be resolved harmoniously.

Occasionally, we sense in our hearts that as soon as we open our mouths, the confrontation is going to get ugly. Having assertive language and a forceful attitude are usually acceptable but when it degenerates into name-calling, abusive tones, and purposeful antagonism, confrontation becomes weighed in the balance in that one will question its necessity. Most tend to shy from any interaction that could escalate into a hostile situation. As unpleasant as it is, sometimes we are forced by circumstances to deal with issues. Jesus was no stranger to confrontation, whether it was telling Peter that his attitude was in league with Satan (Mark 8:33), or when he was having one of his many clashes with the religious leaders of his day. Jesus said hard things that got him into trouble with the ruling elite. Initially, the confrontations were simply verbal and unfriendly. Then they became more intense in their nature and meaning, until they boiled over to argumentative and harsh. His main opposition came from those who saw him as a threat. Confrontation tends to make us tense, jittery, and on edge. These are not the feelings one prefers to have.

He confronted his disciples' lack of understanding, such as the time he rebuked James and John for wanting to call down fire from heaven because some didn't receive him (Luke 9:54-55). He confronted Satan during his temptation in the wilderness and overcame his own thoughts and emotions over the issue of going to the cross.

Paying Taxes

In one confrontation with the Pharisees (Matthew 22:17-21), they asked if it was right to pay the imperial tax to Caesar. Jesus replied, "Give back to Caesar what is Caesar's, and to God what is God's." That signified those taxes did belong to Caesar, in essence, they belonged to the government, the very societal structure that God had ordained (1 Peter 2:13-17, Romans 13:1-5). At one time, Peter mentioned to Jesus their obligation to pay a tax and Jesus gave instruction on where to get the money (Matthew 17:24-27), proving that he would abide by the taxation policy by paying what was due.

Office And Workplace Politics

Jesus had a leadership group; some would say they were his management team. No team or workgroup can live in unity forever. In Mark 9:33-35, they had argued over who was the greatest among them. It would be interesting to hear the criteria they used...was it who was the oldest, who was called by Jesus first, who gave the most money? What rationale did they argue? Were some taking sides with others? Was it a free-for-all? In that account, Jesus handles it privately, inside "the house" or organization or group. Upper management needs to exercise discretion in correction of subordinates.

In any team are those who exceed expectations and those who underperform, at least in comparison to others on the team. The standard for performance, or who is the greatest, must be measured by the contributions of individuals toward the team's goals. In the workplace, friendly competition can be healthy, but when rivalries develop, the team's goals or vision can be vulnerable due to the lack of unity. At times the whole team can get sidetracked. In Mark 10:13-14, the disciples rebuked people who were bringing little children to be blessed, but Jesus corrected the situation by informing that the kingdom of God also belongs to children.

Another incident, involving nepotism, was when the mother of James and John, disciples who already had a considerable "in" with the team leader, was essentially asking Jesus to give her sons a promotion. The other disciples were indignant that she was making such a brazen attempt to get her sons up the corporate ladder (Matthew 20:20-24). Was it jealousy? Was it pride or arrogance? No matter how you slice it, God knows what it is to manage and deal with all the drama of office politics.

Growing A Workforce Ministry

Whether you are a supervisor, manager, or oversee a private business with just a few workers or a large enterprise with thousands, Christ knows what it is to keep tabs on your area of responsibility as a manager of an organization and he also understands what it takes to grow and organize an enterprise. With the disciples, he started out with Andrew (John 1:35-42), who recruited his brother Simon Peter. They then add to their ranks Philip and Nathanael (John 1:43-49). In Luke 5:1-11, while Jesus seems to be alone teaching, although people crowded around to hear him; there, he then adds commitments from Simon, James, and John. In Mark 2:13-14, he builds his team by calling Matthew (also known as Levi) into the fold. Finally in Mark 3:14 we find that Jesus appointed his twelve designating them to be apostles. Jesus then had the inner/upper management team formulated. Leadership was in place; the work was exploding, and all kinds of people had signed on as followers. They got organized and were assigned responsibilities. The demands of a white-collar executive in charge were experienced by Jesus at a human level. A vibrant and exciting new work had invaded the culture. Cutting-edge events were happening, and over-the-top encounters had now promoted Jesus to the top of his field. He went from an unknown to a model to be emulated. In Luke 10:1, he appointed seventy-two others to mid-level management. Kingdom leadership growth has continued unabated for more than two thousand years. There will be no public stock offering; the venture remains as a private enterprise in the non-profit sector. All are invited to participate.

Humanity and Limitations

We all have physical bodies with limitations. The best athletes in the world will eventually reach their own limits. You can run, swim, jump, ski, wrestle, box, and dance fast and far, but only for so long. The human body can be trained for incredible extremes such as heat and cold or for amazing feats of physical accomplishment. Putting our minds into the effort, along with a willing spirit, propels us into areas beyond the norm. Professional athletes have trained for top-notch performances, and it is proven that when faced with a stress-induced challenge, our body's regular limitations can be exceeded. Yet, with all that, no matter what, at some point each body will "hit a wall" and cannot go any farther. Food and drink will be needed for nourishment and rejuvenation. Stress will have to be eliminated and rest applied for recovery. In the normal course of everyday living, we sustain our physical humanity by want and need. Usually, we satisfy the "want" before it becomes a need. Simply by being alive we all require food, water, and rest. The body functions and has needs, whether big or small.

We acknowledge the deity of Christ being one-hundred percent God. This parcel of print will glance at the physicality of Jesus as being one hundred percent man, having his humanity and limitations. Matthew 4:2 states that he was hungry after he fasted for forty days. Who wouldn't be? That incident reveals that God got hungry. Christ understands what it is to go without food and to feel the pangs of that most human need. In Matthew 9:10, Jesus had dinner at Matthew's house and others came and ate with him. He wasn't a stranger to sitting down with others and breaking bread. Another account, in Matthew 21:18, tells us that early in the morning he was hungry. The body has needs. Putting nutrition into it is part of being human. In that instance, Jesus looked at the fig tree for sustenance. God had to receive from the Earth that he created in order to uphold his own body. It is acknowledged in scripture that God identifies with us in our hunger and food issues. He knows what it is to want and need to eat.

John 4:7 finds Jesus requesting a drink from the well in which the Samaritan woman was fetching water. In John 19:28, as he was being brutalized and tortured, the physical demands on his body forced him to make this declaration -- "I am thirsty." God knows what it is to be parched, for a body to not only crave water or food but for that body to be taken to its outer limits into a despairing state of being. Christ understands the dryness accompanying an output of energy. In Luke 7:34, Jesus says to his critics, "The Son of Man came eating and drinking and you say, 'Here is a glutton and a drunkard, a friend of tax collectors and sinners.'" Eating and drinking is both something we do for social activity and for necessity.

That same retelling from John 4:6, "Jesus, tired as he

was from the journey, sat down by the well." Here we find evidence that God understands what it is to expend energy and grow weary. We all get tired from the work and travails of life. Jesus was no exception. Because he lived as one of us, "God as man" had to take a break. Sleepy, droopy eyes, aching muscles, sore feet and a body that wanted to shut down and get some desired rest. Three gospels record Jesus' sleeping in a boat during a storm (Matthew 8:23-24, Mark 4:37-38, and Luke 8:22-24). What wears us out? What wore Jesus out? Could it be simply that he was human and ran up against his normal limitations? That rest was demanded by his earthly body. This wasn't just relaxation; this was out-and-out sleeping. His disciples had to wake him up so they could alert him to the danger around. God knows what it is to reach physical limits because of our humanity. As one of us, he was hungry and ate, he was thirsty and drank, and he got tired and slept. Does God really understand our humanity and limitations? The evidence proves the answer to be "Yes."

Traveling

"Tired as he was from the journey ...," states part of John 4:6. Jesus traveled extensively, from town to town and village to village (Luke 8:1). He traveled for the work he did. God knows what it is to be in the road all the time, at least for a season of your life. He used good old shoe leather which was the main transportation mode of his day. He also had been known to ride on the back of a donkey (Matthew 21:7). He traveled in a boat many times. God knows what it is to have a destination to get to and a message to get out. He traveled alone early on and then with a group. Some people's career path keeps them on the road.

Homelessness

In Matthew 8:20, Jesus states, "Foxes have holes and birds of the air have nests, but the Son of Man has no place to lay his head." Jesus had many supporters and he stayed at different homes, but he didn't have a place of his own. He had forsaken everything for his mission, and it cost him family relationships (more on that in another section), and in some ways, he was not welcomed. He certainly wasn't building equity on investment property or spending money on a principal residence. Not having a place of your own means that you become dependent on the largesse of others to shelter you, or it costs something from your finances for temporary housing. "Has no place to lay his head" indicates that he didn't have any sort of home, not even a room rented out somewhere. Homelessness - - Yes! God understands it.

Funding Sources

It is understood that Jesus was a carpenter. Just as

his earthly father, Joseph, was a carpenter and according to tradition, a firstborn son carried on his father's trade. Matthew 13:55, "Isn't this the carpenter's son?" Mark 6:3, "Isn't this the carpenter?" It's reasonable to expect that Jesus plied his trade and made a living for himself and his family until he went into ministry, around 30 years of age. In other words, he worked for his dad in the family business until his dad passed away, (the rationale) then he became self-employed. After perhaps fifteen years or more of this blue-collar work, he set out on his own and started a nonprofit organization that derived its funding from the charitable donations of those who supported his work. Luke 8:3 states that "These women were helping to support them out of their own means." This is reiterated in Mark 15:41, "In Galilee these women had followed him and cared for his needs." Traveling costs money, and the funding was provided by those who believed in him. God understands what it is to be dependent on others for funding sources.

Being Normal

Later, Chapter 7 on Celebrity covers the "lifestyle of the rich and/or famous." Most would say there was never anything normal about the earthly life of Christ. Admittedly, most of his recorded life was anything but normal but there was a timeframe from a young child to 12 years of age that is silent, and from 12 years of age to when he went public. In the next section, regarding family life, I'll cover known events during those periods, but these portions of his life are unrecorded. We get a total of around five to six years of written information. What about the other years? What attracted people to Jesus after age 30 were his teachings and his exercise of spiritual gifts. If he was walking down the street before his public period, no one would have thought twice about him. He would have fit in as a completely normal human being. Isaiah 53:2 speaks about the normalcy of Christ, "He had no beauty or majesty to attract us to him, nothing in his appearance that we should desire him." He wasn't exceptionally anything. He wasn't extra tall or short, heavy or thin, or handsome or ugly. He was "Joe Average." A normal "Joe Shmoe" who might not have gotten a second glance from the cute maidens or been the first pick for classroom president. Nothing about his exterior suggested specialness for the future. There was nothing about his appearance, demeanor, or the way he carried himself that spoke out of his divine purpose. When he walked around in the non-public years, he was an overlooked and unnoticed persona. More of the life of Christ was spent being and living normally than not. Does God understand what it is to be normal? Yes!

Family Life

It's simple reality that Jesus had Joseph and Mary as his earthly mother and father. We can honestly say that God knows what it is to have parents. Joseph's father was Jacob

(Matthew 1:15-16). How well Jesus knew his grandparents on either side is conjecture, but it seems reasonable that he would have been familiar with them along with whatever aunts, uncles, and cousins. In growing up, he would have been nursed, potty trained; taught to walk, communicate, read, write, dress, and bathe himself like any other child. How do you get to be 12? You first get to 10. Before 10 you are 8; before you're 8, you are 5; before you are 5, you are 2, and so on. At 12, many know the story of Jesus' temporary separation from his parents (Luke 2:41-46), but verse 44 states that they were traveling with relatives and friends. The key point here is that Jesus had relatives of some nature.

In a visit to his hometown, the people declared in response to his ministry, "Isn't this the carpenter's son?" (Matthew 13:54-57), and in Mark 6:1-3 the people remarked that Jesus himself was the carpenter. The family issue in those passages is the recognition of his siblings; his brothers James, Joseph, Simon, Judas (four listed), and his sisters. Matthew states "all his sisters," implying more than two. At this point he had four brothers and what appears to be at least three sisters being a reasonable calculation. Seven siblings, plus he as the oldest, brings the total to eight. Let's consider this practical calculation: If Mary and Joseph had a child born every two and one-half years on average, then Jesus would have been almost 18 years old when the possible last child was born. Jesus as a 12-year-old would have had siblings ages 9½, 7, 4½, 2, and "one in the oven." For many years, Jesus was in a house full of little kids: diapers, nursing, crying and carrying on; runny noses all over the place, playing, fighting and screaming. Being the oldest probably meant assignments of responsibility for the brood. As Jesus grew in age, his voice would have deepened, muscles developed, and facial hair would have appeared; yes, God understands puberty and what it is to be a teenager and sibling. The sibling group grew in age along with their numbers. With a steady supply of teenagers, Jesus witnessed sibling rivalry, jealousy, teen angst—the list goes on. Luke 3:23 states that Jesus was about 30 when he started his ministry. Using similar calculations, that would put his siblings' ages at approximately 27½, 25, 22½, 20, 17½, 15, and 12½; his siblings would have been young adults and teenagers. It's extremely plausible that some were married, and he had in-law siblings of some nature, perhaps even having nephews and nieces.

At 30 Jesus started his ministry and he was a wildly successful at it yet in Mark 6:1-4 we see problems surface with family life. Jesus makes the claim in verse 4: "Only in his hometown, among his relatives and in his own house, is a prophet without honor." You can reach the mountaintop in your profession and those closest to you either can't accept it, or don't recognize it, the same way as everyone else does. It got so bad for Jesus that in Mark 3:21, his family went to take charge of him because they thought he had gone out of his mind. His family (mainly his brothers) came to shut him down. They came to talk some sense into him and to deprogram him. At that point, his brothers didn't believe in him or his work. This wasn't sibling rivalry; it was staging an intervention for his perceived own good. Practically no one he grew up with - - neighbors, community associates, siblings, or childhood friends - - gave him their backing. The family thought he had "gone dysfunctional" on them and was dragging others down with him. Does God understand family drama? You bet!

Sometimes it simply takes time and patience for family to come around. Acts 1:14 relates that all his disciples were gathered in prayer and Mary, the mother of Jesus and his earthly siblings, gathered as one with them. Who wrote the books of James and Jude? It was his half-brothers who came to believe in him. God was born a human baby, weaned as a child, grew as a teenager in small-town life, developed into a man, had relatives, parents, siblings, and family issues. Does God really understand family life? Yes!

Adultery

There is no doubt that this subject is related to betrayal, injustice, rejection, and perhaps desertion (B. I. R. D further explained in Chapter 8), yet adultery is so significant in its destruction that it needs to be examined as a topic by itself. This is a heavy hitter, like the death of a loved one. Does

God really understand adultery? How could he when he's never been married? Let's investigate what God has to say about adultery since it affected him personally. God is quoted in Jeremiah 3:8 as saying, "I gave faithless Israel her certificate of divorce and sent her away because of her adulteries." Blatantly, Israel is personified as a woman ("her"), God divorces "her" because of her adulteries (plural, many adulteries). In God's view, she was a repeat offender, and you can't divorce someone from whom you weren't in a marriage bond. Reading on in Jeremiah 3:14, "Return faithless people,' declares the Lord, 'for I am your husband." What an analogy is being made! God is recognizing himself as in a marriage. He takes this seriously as every married partner should. In this scripture, it's apparent that he still seeks reconciliation. Moving forward to Jeremiah 3:20, God continues his scrutiny with this – "But like a woman unfaithful to her husband, so you have been unfaithful to me, O house of Israel,' declares the Lord."

This becomes for blunt and direct. Jeremiah 5:7 reads, "Why should I forgive you? Your children have forsaken me and sworn by gods that are not gods. I supplied all their needs, yet they committed adultery and thronged to the houses of prostitutes." God's identity in this is as husband, father, provider, family man and committed member of the relationship, and now he's the victim of divorce by no fault of his own.

Ezekiel 16 has as its basis a discourse on Jerusalem as

God's unfaithful wife. Verse 20 reads, "And you took your sons and daughters whom you bore to me and sacrificed them as food to the idols. Was your prostitution not enough?" This shows God's identification as a husband and father. Children are always the victims of wayward parents. God was lamenting the degree of hurt and pain as being promoted by the unfaithfulness of a marriage partner. Verse 32 reads, "You adulterous wife! You prefer strangers to your own husband!" This is an ugly and pain filled comparison that God is having from the position of a husband who has been betrayed. I stand in opposition to anyone who wants to take away from this description as a sordid affair because God himself is making the comparison. It is God who used this language, had this viewpoint, and who cast the perspective, attitudes, and disparagement. This wasn't God drawing up an analogy or identity marker to feel one with mankind, this was true expression of similar pain and agony of an unfaithful spouse and a resulting divorce. This is God's indictment because of reality.

In verse 32, God states that all cultural norms were being crossed and he was getting the "raw end of the deal." His children had been turned against him (Jeremiah 5:7) and taken from him (Ezekiel 16:20). All priorities had been turned upside down. In the dismantling of a covenant relationship, such as marriage, usually there is some degree of fault on both sides, but in God's case, the pain and loss were one-sided in that his partner exercised no discretion or restraint in abusing him with her public and profane practices which added "insult to injury." As God was experiencing adultery on more than one occasion.

The book of Hosea is illustrative of adulterous Israel, as the prophet married an adulterous wife. Hosea 1:2 is probably the single most informative statement about God's outlook on the matter. It reads, "When the Lord began to speak through Hosea, the Lord said to him, 'Go, and take to yourself an adulterous wife, and children of unfaithfulness, because the land is guilty of the vilest adultery in departing from the Lord.'" "The vilest form of adultery" signifies that he had been betrayed in the worst manner possible. Are there differing degrees of adultery? The one-night stand that is repented of or the flagrant continual abusive variety. What would it be like to be married to someone like that? God is saying he's been there; he felt it through and through. In the eyes of God, he suffered through the "bottom of the barrel" type of adultery. God understands the pain, the selfishness, the prolonged heartache, the public humiliation, the children conflict, the sorrow of serving divorce papers as well as the hope of reconciliation. Does God really understand adultery? Yes!

Chapter 6

Does God Really Understand My Emotions?

What are some things that make us angry?

- "He never helps with the housework."

- "She's always nagging for help with the housework."

- "The kids don't listen."

- "The boss expects too much."

- Really bad service when dining out.

- A rude cashier.

- "The car is still acting up even after it's been in the garage and has cost lots of money."

- "Our sports team losing."

- Knowing someone who got killed by a drunk driver.
- Someone telling an embarrassing story about us.
- Losing a big chunk of retirement investment due to mismanagement.
- Someone bullying our kids.

Admittedly, a variety of situations and issues can lead to anger. Sometimes they are seemingly small things; at other times, they are big things. Also, some people are more sensitive than others. We can get in quite an agreement about having a right to get angry, or what some may term "righteous indignation." At other times, a person's response may be overblown in the sense that they are overreacting. Their emotional response of anger is disproportionate to the offense. Maybe, in some cases, a person's anger response level is too low, and it signifies apathy. A person can wear their emotions on their sleeve, revealing a hyper-sensitivity, or they can subdue their emotions to the point of others charging them with being uncaring, cold, or calloused. What is right or wrong about our emotional makeup? What is right or wrong about our emotional responses and reactions?

Depending on what we are going through in any given moment or season of life, our emotions can run all over the place. Remember the saying, "emotions are running high?" Tread lightly when Momma is fretting over her weight issues and how she looks in her clothes! But circumstances play a pivotal role in our emotions. Because we live in our emotions, and judge ourselves with the emotions we are experiencing, it's not wrong to ask the question, Does God really understand what I'm going through as it concerns my emotions?

The first thing we must understand is that God isn't devoid of emotions. We are going to look at a full range of emotions that God has experienced as evidenced by scripture. We'll examine the above-mentioned anger and then look at frustration, disappointment, regret, grief, heartache, pain, sorrow, and crying. Perhaps not an exhaustive list but one that people struggle with, considering that many of these emotions are mischaracterized by the misinformed as ones that Christians should either never experience, or should only experience in temporal fashion and immediately move on to a more positive tone. God himself experienced these emotions, so they are not rooted in immature Christians who just need to "buck up" and somehow transcend themselves to being well-equipped saints who never "lower themselves" to these types of emotions.

Is Anger A Sin?

Is anger a sin? Hopefully, everyone who ever reads this question understands that the answer is "no." Anger, as an emotion in and of itself, is not a sin. The Bible says that we are to not sin in our anger. Ephesians 4:26, "In your anger do not sin." The reality is to not lose control or give up your character and do something rash and unreasonable that would get anyone into trouble, because anger got the best of us. We are now going to prove that God has the emotion of anger, and because God has experienced that emotion, it can almost go without saying that the emotional reaction is not sinful. Exodus 4:14 informs that the Lord's anger burned against Moses. There it is, God got angry with Moses. In that incident, it boiled down to the fact that God had a mission for Moses who was making excuses for why he couldn't get involved and do it.

In Numbers 11:10, we read that the Lord "became exceedingly angry" with the Israelites because of their complaining and dissatisfaction. Reading through Deuteronomy 9:7-24 and counting how many incidents provoked the Lord's anger. In 1 Kings 11:9, the Lord became angry with King Solomon, the wisest, richest man who ever lived, because his heart had turned away from him. In 2 Kings 17:16-18 the Israelites were worshipping idols, practicing child sacrifice, and doing all kinds of evil things which aroused God's anger. In Job 42:7, God informs Eliphaz that he is angry with him and his two friends because they haven't spoken the truth about him. Please read Psalm 78 for an exposé on God's anger and the "why" of it. It attests to God's righteous indignation.

"Righteous indignation" is a right to be angry. An

expectation that you should and will get angry. God showed and revealed that emotion. Unfortunately, many people write off the Old Testament as just the mood swings of an angry, old, testy God, and when his hip son Jesus came along, he changed his attitude to cool and mellow. Firstly, "God changes not" (Malachi 3:6); he is "the same yesterday, today and tomorrow" (Hebrews 13:8). Secondly, if Jesus is our model, let's next look at some moments of his life as they relate to anger.

Jesus Got Angry

Mark 3:1-5 is the account of a man with a shriveled hand which Jesus was going to heal, but because it was the Sabbath, there were those who couldn't, or wouldn't, decide that it was acceptable for Jesus to heal him. Some thought he shouldn't be doing that kind of thing simply because it was the Sabbath. Verse 5 reveals that Jesus looked at them in anger and was deeply distressed at their stubborn hearts. He commanded the man to stretch out his hand, and as he did so, it was healed. It was in that moment, of Jesus' defiance and anger, that the religious opposition decided to plot his death. We understand that God doesn't sin in his anger. yet sometimes, even doing well in our anger, can bring others against us. The bottom line is that Jesus got angry in the New Testament. Peek at John 2:13-17, to the incident where Jesus drove out the moneychangers with a whip and overturned their table. Does that story sound like someone with anger management issues? Or as verse 17 says, "Zeal for God's house consumed him." Anger can take hold of us when we are passionate about something worthwhile that is being misused or abused, and we set ourselves to act. In Revelation 16:1, we are reminded of future events to unfold, when God has seven bowls of wrath that he will pour out on the earth. Wrath signifies great anger; an anger that cannot be appeased until it has been poured out. In John 14:9, Jesus said, "Anyone who has seen me has seen the Father." Remember with whom Jesus was completely identifying. When God's wrath is being poured out, it can legitimately be said that it is the wrath of Christ.

The conclusion is that God can, and does, get angry. The difference is that God doesn't "fly off the handle." He doesn't lose his temper and have a "fit of rage" because he isn't getting his way. God follows his own admonitions such as in James 1:19, "Everyone should be quick to listen, slow to speak, and slow to become angry." God gets angry with individuals (Solomon, Moses), groups (Pharisees), kingdoms, and the world. 1 John 4:16 reveals that God is love. In 1 Corinthians 13:5, we find that love is not easily angered (or offended). The context of scripture is that God is love and because love is not easily angered, God is not easily angered. However, that doesn't mean never angered. God has experienced, and continues to experience, the emotion of anger.

Frustration

What makes us frustrated? It is a relevant question because the next logical step to frustration, is anger. Many times, frustration precedes anger. People get frustrated over all kinds of things, such as not being able to get the lid off the jar, when we can't read the print without our reading glasses, undecipherable tax language, the instruction papers to assemble something, getting a speeding ticket when we honestly didn't see the reduced speed sign, or people who just don't "get it," whatever "it" is. This was Jesus' situation recorded in three Gospels -- Matthew 17:14-18, Mark 9:14-27, and Luke 9:37-43. Summarized, a boy was demon-possessed, the father brought him to the disciples to be healed, and they could not do it. Jesus' response was the same. He said to all of them, "O unbelieving and perverse generation, how long shall I stay with you? How long shall I put up with you?" This is a prime example of God being frustrated over the fact that they were exercising so little faith after he had shown them so much and had done so much. They weren't getting it. Perhaps the most frustrating thing for most of us is when we are trying to help, teach, inform, and lift others up; when we are setting the correct example and they still "fall flat on their faces."

Frustration is always tempered by progress, however done, even in small steps. If we see someone making some type of progress, some degree of forward momentum, however slow or incremental, at least we have hope of "better late than never," or the thought that someday they will get it. Jesus did not "bite his tongue" to not say, "How long shall I stay with you? How long shall I put up with you?" (Mark 9:19). This castigating rebuke revealed God's frustration with them. However, look at the frustration all around. The crowd was disappointed that they didn't get to witness this healing and the boy's father surely experienced great frustration and disappointment at the letdown, especially after repeated attempts by various disciples. The disciples themselves would have experienced frustration as perhaps one after another tried and couldn't heal the boy. Possibly, if the boy had any sense of himself at all, he would have experienced great frustration and disappointment at not being healed and set free. There was plenty of frustration and disappointment to go around, after all, it would have been the disciples' reputation from their association with Jesus for the father to have sought them out for the healing, and for the crowd to have gathered in anticipation. Jesus had previously commissioned the twelve disciples (Matthew 10:1-8) to go out and drive out evil spirits, heal every disease and sickness, heal the sick, raise the dead, cleanse those who have leprosy, and drive out demons. Yet they failed. Jesus got frustrated so that means that God got frustrated. Everyone involved was frustrated and disappointed.

Frustration And Disappointment

Frustration and disappointment are closely related. Does God get disappointed? Isn't he supposed to have a happy face on all the time? Happy, happy, joy, joy. The retelling in Matthew 14:22-31 is of Peter's walking on the water and becoming afraid. Sinking in the water, he calls out to Jesus (smart move!) and Jesus catches him. Jesus' response was one of disappointment as he said, "You of little faith, why did you doubt?" It was obvious that Christ wanted Peter to continue to walk on the water ... to go the distance with him and not be afraid. Instead, Peter failed in this instance. God is terribly disappointed that we take our eyes off him and lose our courage to endure or lose our chance at succeeding at something great. When we examine situations and realize the better path, or better result of choices that could have been made but weren't; then disappointment becomes the reality of our emotions. Disappointment at how things turn out. The letdown of anticipation, the unfulfilled expectation, a yearning and longing that stays just that.

Frustration and disappointment are not exclusive to us. Even Christ experienced these emotions. How often does God experience that emotion today? He wants his children to love one another, prefer one another, and forgive one another; be kind, holy, loyal to him, biblically literate, financially giving; yet we fail him, sometimes miserably, especially if the failure becomes more intense or unrepentantly long-term. How often do we feel frustrated with others who have character defects, or disappointment over those who refuse to move forward in Christian growth, and in some cases, do the proverbial backslide into moral failure?

We can move from frustration and disappointment to anger and indignation. How much more so for God? God has feelings also; feelings toward his children -- frustration, disappointment, anger -- all these emotions are not necessarily negative but can be indicative of someone who cares and values the relationships that these feelings are directed toward. If someone didn't care about your progress and well-being, then they wouldn't really be disappointed. Perhaps they would be again: apathetic, or uncaring, but God cares enough to let himself feel and experience these emotions over you. He asks, "What could have been for my child; what still can be for my child?"

Regrets, Grief, And Heartache

Can an awesome, all-powerful, all-knowing God experience these emotions? Let's refer to Genesis 6:5-6, "The Lord saw how great man's wickedness on the earth had become, and that every inclination of the thoughts of his heart was only evil all the time. The Lord was grieved that he had made man on the earth, and his heart was filled with pain." Have you ever been involved in something in an important way, perhaps at the ground level, and things went south? I don't mean obstacles or setbacks to your end goal, but you accomplished something of significance; it was a noteworthy endeavor that deserved accolades and recognition and, through a twist of fate or because of someone's actions, especially if that someone was a beneficiary of your effort, the whole thing came apart or was basically brought to ruin or insignificance? God created mankind and all was well for a time. Through someone's failure, a chain of events was set into motion that filled the whole earth with wickedness. God understands having regrets over something that's happened. There you are, with all the best intentions and expectations in the world, and others come along and ruin everything! God was grieved that he had made man. He was terribly upset over how bad the situation had become. God knew, that at that moment in time, there were no redeeming traits left in his work. His creation had gone in a totally different direction than was expected, and bad-to-worse had become worse-to-unrecoverable. This occurrence was grieving to God, and it filled his heart with pain.

How sad it is when we do our part, like God, to make things right, and others destroy our efforts and their own lives in the process. The circumstances, sometimes for us and as always with God, are that there were no mistakes made by him. He had not committed sin or offenses. It wasn't his fault! Even active involvement and doing our part to maintain the wheels that are set in motion, won't have the results we're looking for, when others are set against our vision and ideas. Another example of God grieving and having regret is told in 1 Samuel 15:11 where God says to the prophet Samuel, "I am grieved that I have made Saul king because he has turned away from me and has not carried out my instructions." In the earlier mentioned Genesis 6 scripture, God is grieved over a group, essentially all of mankind. In the latter 1 Samuel reference, he is grieved over one individual. God's regrets go just as deep no matter the number; it's the outcome that matters. Saul was pretty much a nobody before God made him King. However, Saul wouldn't obey God like he should have, and could have, and God was upset in his behavior to the point that he regretted his decision to give him a chance. How many times have people been given a chance to prove themselves, whether in promotion, leadership, or projects, and because they won't follow the rules, thus their leader begins having regrets in having chosen that person?

The question goes begging, did God make a mistake? No, God doesn't make mistakes or sin. Rather, God gives people, groups, and individuals the chance to succeed, to improve, and to fail. When they don't succeed or improve, he often gives them more time and more chances. Remember, he is not the God of only a second chance; he is the God of another chance.

Admittedly, there came a point at which God had to say, "enough is enough." For groups and individuals, God, in his regret, heartache, and pain, had to move on. He had given multiple chances, over a period, proving that He exercised great patience. Ephesians 4:30, "And do not grieve the Holy Spirit of God, with whom you were sealed for the day of redemption." Again, this proves that God can be grieved. Typically, that is accomplished by our living lives contrary to the expectations and directions of our creator and savior. Remembering that God is love, and that love is not easily offended (1 Corinthians 13:1), does not mean that Love (God) can't be offended. He can be and is offended when the love he has for us, which is so strong, brings him grief when we are not where we could be spiritually. Whereas frustration is more like heartburn; grieving is more like heartache.

Multiple Emotions

About what do people grieve? What causes heartache outside of death or disappointment? We all understand the emotions of regret and grieving. Take, for example, a troubled or failed marriage. Perhaps we grow to realize that we should have waited to marry or that we married the wrong person. Maybe going to Vegas single, not knowing anyone, then waking up with a hangover and a wedding ring with no clue of what happened the previous night, is not in our best interest. Doing the impulsive and impetuous has a higher risk factor of regret than careful deliberation. Having a go-it-alone mindset that doesn't seek out advice from others, especially from experts, can increase our chances of regret. Regrets, and the associated grieving, take many forms. From overeating binges and lack of exercise, to lying out in the sun too long without adequate sunscreen. From the child who doesn't want a baby sibling competing for family attention, to the senior citizen in their twilight season reviewing episodes of their life they wish they could go back and reconstruct. From the doctor who prescribed the wrong medicine to their patient's detriment, to the teenager who sacrificed their virginity on a whim. Consider the regrets of parents who, after counseling their children out of their experienced wisdom, watch them make the same mistakes they made and are having to live with the same consequences. Or, seeing a loved one in some type of addiction like drugs, alcohol, gambling, or pornography; watching them decay themselves and destroy relationships because of these unhealthy choices that led to destructive lifestyles. We can love someone and at the same time be upset with them, still. committed to their wellbeing while angry, frustrated, disappointed, having regrets, grieving, and experiencing heartache. Sound familiar as a life experience?

As a rule of thumb, people experience these emotions because they care about the people involved, the situation or, both. We can have multiple emotions in simultaneous fashion, just like God who created us. This has us following in the emotional footsteps of God who went through these predicaments before us. You can love someone and still be angry with them. You can feel multiple emotions about them and their circumstances.

Sorrow

Many scholars believe that the first verse of Isaiah 53:1-13 concerns itself prophetically with the life of Christ. Verse 2 reveals, "He grew up before him like a tender shoot, and like a root out of dry ground. He had no beauty or majesty to attract us to him, nothing in his appearance that we should desire him." A tender shoot is unnoticed simply because it grows just like the others, perfectly normal with no outstanding characteristics, growing up and maturing like everyone else, always average with no discernible gifts, talents, or attractions. And that's OK! How many of us live a mundane life? "Mr., Mrs., or Miss Joe Average," happy to be a part of boredom, which can sometimes be a synonym for stability. Whoever said that life had to have consistent crisis or be fast paced? What's wrong with the status quo? What's so special about being a root out of dry ground? Nothing! There's nothing wrong with humble beginnings (Zechariah 4:10). Jesus was born in a lowly manger, an animal trough. As he grew, he didn't have any outstanding qualities that set him apart from others. When Saul was appointed king, he was described as a head taller than other men (1 Samuel 9:2). When David was anointed king, the description was that he was a ruddy-looking boy with bright eyes and good-looking; in other words, handsome (1 Samuel 16:12 NKJV). Jesus was never described with any of these qualities. No beauty or majesty, no big money supply; a so-called nobody, happily fitting into the crowd, at least for the early season of his life. There was nothing of a physical or outstanding nature to attract us to him. God had nothing special in his appearance as a human, Jesus. God understands commonality. He wasn't tall, or handsome, or overtly appealing, especially in any physical sense. Most of us aren't. God can relate to being typical, common, and ordinary. Isaiah 53:3, "He was despised and rejected by men, a man of sorrows, and familiar with suffering." More on the rejection issue later, but let's consider the idea of a man of sorrows, familiar with suffering. Anyone with any degree of love and compassion for others would certainly be moved by the plight of those whom they loved. Carrying the thought that God is love, and that God loves us, and that many reject that love, it is only logical that because God so loved the world, that when he sent his son to save it and so many rejected him, it was grieving and brought with it a consistent sorrow. This is not to say that Jesus walked around in his life never laughing or smiling, but a man of sorrows would have a heart condition, a soulful familiarity at his inner core with not just physical suffering, but emotional and mental suffering, brought on by "The

BIRD," an acronym further explained in Chapter 8 that stands for Betrayal, Injustice, Rejection, and Desertion.

Some people live lives that have dealt them a stream of harshness and difficulty. In some cases, those difficulties may have been brought on by poor choices, someone else's poor choices, or nothing more than bad circumstances such as being in the wrong place at the wrong time. Jesus' life shows that he didn't make poor choices. It can be persuasively argued that he had joy, especially the joy of the Lord! His emotions would have a component of sorrow within its scope or range.

Pushed To Tears

Crying is a manifestation of our emotions. Sometimes we cry from being overjoyed; we just got married, the baby is born, or we bought our first home. We cry when we win (the war is over), when we have overcome (the cancer is gone), or we accomplish something (the diploma is in hand). Usually, we cry out of emotions of sorrow, grief, anger, and such. John 11:1-44 reveals the story of the death of Lazarus. Lazarus dies and ultimately Jesus raises him from the dead. but the story within the story is that Lazarus has two sisters, and Jesus loved all three of them. When Jesus arrives on the scene, Mary, one of the sisters, goes out to meet him." When Jesus saw her weeping and the Jews who had come along with her also weeping, he was deeply moved in spirit and troubled. 'Where have you laid him?' he asked. 'Come and see, Lord,' they replied. Jesus wept. Then the Jews said, 'See how much he loved him!'" This was not a false accusation; it was a moment of truth.

God, as Jesus, wept and mourned for someone he loved, and he wept alongside those he loved. He was influenced and moved by their loss and grief. People are moved to tears by their emotional identification. Consider how many people cry over movies and television; the depiction of a love won, lost, and then recovered in romances. There are heart-to-heart issues relating over fiction and reality that move people so much emotionally that they release that emotion through tears. How many tears are shed at funerals? This biblical example of weeping was at Lazarus' funeral. How many tears are shed at weddings? (I could get a lot of mileage out of some bad jokes about crying over getting married, but I'll move on.) People cry at hospitals, graduations, and send-offs. We cry over what affects us directly and what doesn't affect us at all yet touches us emotionally.

When the Jews observed how much Jesus loved Lazarus, they knew the tears that Jesus shed were not based on identifying with a fictional character but were the "real deal" of someone feeling the pain of others as well as feeling their own pain. God, as Jesus, cried. He shed real tears over a real situation. He understands the emotions that demand the release of tears. and he also understands the tears we shed from our emotions.

The bible has many stories of godly people crying. A man named Joseph, sold into slavery by his brothers, became second in command in Egypt. His brothers came into Egypt seeking help and when they appeared before him, they didn't recognize him, but he recognized them. After a while, he made himself known to them and was reunited, with many tears (Genesis 45:1-2). Another example is in the book of Ruth who basically starts out with a woman named Naomi who moved to a foreign land with her husband and two sons and then all three died. Naomi is left with her two daughters-in-law and decides to go back to Israel and have them return to their original families. At the departure, they wept over their losses and no longer being together (Ruth 1:9, 14). A woman named Hannah (1 Samuel 1:1-10) wept in bitterness of soul over not being able to have a child. King David fasted and wept over his newborn son who was dying (2 Samuel 12:21-22). Another king named Hezekiah (2 Kings 20:1-5) is known to have wept bitterly over learning of the news of his impending death and prayed for recovery. God said that he had heard his prayer, saw Hezekiah's tears, and would heal him. When a godly man named Nehemiah heard of the distress of his people, and that Jerusalem was falling into disrepair, he sat down and wept, mourned, fasted, and prayed (Nehemiah 1:3-4). Apostle Peter, whom Jesus prophesied would deny him three times before the rooster crowed, to which Peter said never! After it happened, he went outside and broke down and wept bitterly (Matthew 26:75, Mark 14:72, and Luke 22:61-62). Another godly man, who wrote the Book of Revelation, was named John. In describing a vision (Chapter 5:1-9) he finds himself in heaven with no one worthy to open the scroll held in the right hand of he who sits on the throne (God). This dilemma caused the writer to weep until he was informed that there was someone, the Lamb who had been slain, Jesus Christ.

Our emotions force the tears of expression. Tears may represent different emotions, at different points in time, for different circumstances. Jesus cried more than once. Another incident involving tears is found in Luke 19:41. As Jesus approached Jerusalem at the triumphal entry, he was moved to tears over what was going to happen to Jerusalem; the people, and the spiritual reality that they had missed the opportunity to gain real peace. However, two things should be pointed out about this occurrence. The original Greek word for wept is Klaio, which means "to wail, or hard crying (extreme), as in a lamentation." This was no single-teardrop moment. This was done in front of everyone around him, his disciples, the crowds along the road, and even his detractors. In front of everyone, God as Jesus breaks down and prophesies in tears. He needed to release his emotions; he stops everything and, so to speak, "loses it." God has emotions and so do we. God, as human, needed to release his emotions through tears. Sometimes so do we. It's okay to have emotions. Be reminded that the bible states in Ecclesiastes 3:4, "there is a time to weep." If you find yourself in that state, it's okay! It's okay to have, feel, confess, release, and live out your emotions, even with tears, just as Jesus did.

Chapter 7

Celebrity

The Greatest Celebrity Who Ever Lived And Still Does, Is Jesus Christ.

One of the great dreams of many is to be a recognized persona in the public arena. Some may have dreams of being a famous athlete in a specific field. Some may dream of being a great boxer, wrestler, dancer, swimmer, football or soccer player, or volleyball champion. Others may want to be a champion race car driver or excel in motocross or boating. Even others may have a secret desire to be a world-class ballerina, a karate master, a best-selling author, or a grand master at the game of chess. Gaining attention from the public may spur some to seek the opportunities and develop the requisite expertise. Some seek that place through music, whether it be composing or performing. A public personality in the entertainment genre is what most would desire. "To be, or not to be (that is the question!" – William Shakespeare), an actor; to sing on Broadway; to star in a hit TV series or movie. One reason is that with celebrity recognition, usually money, and ego-satisfying identity are achieved. Others seek public or popular identities as politicians, running for office as community leaders, which may give way to aspirations for higher desires, perhaps Senators, Governors, or President.

The styles may differ, the roads to get there may vary, but those driven by ambition and aptitude are better candidates for achievement than those who only dream and never do anything to achieve that dream. We all read or hear about celebrities and the lives they lead. We have a romantic notion of what it would be like to have fame and fortune. To have people clamoring to get our autograph, to shout our name, and generally to have enough money to do what we want when we want to do it. Two things need to be acknowledged. For most, celebrity didn't come without a price, especially for the athlete or movie star. The second is that no matter what, sometimes it boils down to being in the right place at the right time, or as it is said, the luck of the draw. However, the person who recognizes and makes the most of their opportunity is still doing their part. Face it - - It doesn't matter if someone has opportunity if they can't or won't fulfill the expectations of that opportunity. Some navigate celebrity well; others have a hard time coping and fail miserably at it. Celebrity can be characterized as notoriety. Those successful at it continue doing what got them there, and that's what usually keeps them there.

How many would welcome everything that goes with being a celebrity? Too often a celebrity has a meltdown in front of the cameras that follow them, when it was the cameras, they sought to begin with. Being famous is what was wanted, and many times the crowds that are needed to keep them famous, are resisted by the celebrities themselves. It's perfectly understandable at its core; the celebrity must have some space, as we all do. But in looking at celebrities, what comparisons can be made with the life of Christ?

Quite a bit. The question is asked, "Does God really understand celebrity?" While he was still quite young, and his parents had moved on to Jerusalem, wise men (magi) from the East came to bring him gifts and to worship him because they recognized his star (could we call this his "star power?"). They called him the King of the Jews. A celebrity had been born! This account is found in Matthew 2:1-12.

The Principle That Celebrity Is Built Upon

We are now going to look at some scriptures that give us insight into Jesus' world of celebrity. By no means is it exhaustive; here are some highlights. John 2:23-24, "Now while he was in Jerusalem at the Passover Feast, many people saw the miraculous signs he was doing and believed in his name. But Jesus would not entrust himself to them, for he knew all men." This is one of the first examples of Jesus' popularity and rising star status. It was the consequence of people seeing his miracles and being impressed with his efforts and results. Isn't this the principle that much of celebrity is built upon? We notice what someone's doing and what they're all about, we like what we see, we can relate, and in some manner, they're fulfilling a need or want of ours, whether actual or fantasized.

The role of the celebrity to the fans or admirers is in the eye of the beholders. They fulfill actual or fantasized needs or wants in some measure and, therefore, receive devotees. Jesus was fulfilling actual needs and it promoted his status to that of celebrity. Yet Verse 24 reveals that "Jesus would not entrust himself to them, for he knew all men." In other words, they weren't going to become confidants and trusted advisors as Christ understood that the court of public opinion could become exceptionally fickle. One minute, someone is the toast of the town, and the next, they're yesterday's news. Ask any has-been entertainer, the lesson learned is that Jesus kept his head about the truth of crowds. He kept his reality check in place as soon as the crowds and the pace picked up in "Celebrityville."

Luke 4:14-15, "Jesus returned to Galilee in the power of the Spirit, and news about him spread through the whole countryside. He taught in their synagogues, and everyone praised him." Celebrity can bring with it access otherwise not known. When the people want to be around you, it can open doors to venues that might not normally be available. News about Jesus spread; the best advertising is by word of mouth. When someone we know well, informs us of an experience they had, it usually beats out in importance, a newspaper advertisement. Of course, back in that day they didn't have any form of electronic social media and the main way of communicating was personal communication. At that time, the word about "The Word" was spreading. Jesus was doing things that attracted people and kept them coming back, the main principle behind celebrity. Jesus was now moving from a niche market and was starting to go mainstream. He was finding an audience among the greater population, sort of like going from local community broadcasting to regional recognition, and everyone praised him. He was being accepted for what he represented. He was finding formal outlets for his ministry. His efforts were now going beyond the localized circuit and morphing into greater mass appeal.

Later in his travels, Jesus was in a synagogue and cast out a demon. The people were amazed. Luke 5:15, "And the news about him spread throughout the surrounding area." When someone has something that others want and/or need, that brings their attraction. When that person travels from place to place, their reputation increases and is magnified. Jesus' renown was picking up everywhere he traveled. In each region, people talked of his deeds.

His work was becoming more and more prominent. He continued to do his work, and Matthew 4:24 reveals, "News about him spread all over Syria," and his popularity soared.

Luke 4:42 is a telling scripture: "At daybreak, Jesus went out to a solitary place. The people were looking for him and when they came to where he was, they tried to keep him from leaving them." There comes a point when no one can sustain living in the limelight and they need to get away, regroup and clear their head and evaluate life as it really is; to prepare for the future and pray about it all. Even when Jesus was seeking a little bit of downtime, people were looking for him. Celebrities can't always find alone time when others are intentionally on the hunt for their whereabouts. Verse 42 informs that they tried to keep him from leaving them. It's one thing for fans to wear a T-shirt, hang a poster, or get an autograph so that, in a vicarious way, the famous person doesn't leave us, but it's a different situation to want that person to stay. While it's not wrong to want to persuade someone to spend more time with us, there does come that moment when we all need to move on.

What happens when renown becomes so big that their celebrity is known just about everywhere they go, and they can no longer walking around freely without recognition? This is a dream of many, to have their face and name in the "big city lights," or to have that pop-star persona; to be a household name. Jesus came to such a position in his society. Mark 1:45 indicates that because of the news about him, "Jesus could no longer enter a town openly but stayed outside in lonely places. Yet the people still came to him from everywhere." One of the things that we all value is some degree of privacy. How 'wonderful' would it be, each time you went into a restaurant, that people would crowd you especially when you have a mouthful of food, or just wanted to spend some time dining out with family without a barrage of interruptions? How about if you had to use the restroom? I shudder at that one!

The Key To Sanity

Some celebrities disguise themselves, so no one recognizes them, yet to be renown is what many sought to begin with. When they can't get through an airport line or checkout without people crowding them for attention, or try on clothes without the clamor of others, let alone take a vacation but not enjoy the hotspots or highlights because they become the center of attention for those people who think they're on vacation with the celebrity, who has now become their hotspot and highlight. What a conundrum -- seeking to be a celebrity and then becoming a victim of their own success. How to deal with this reality? Everyone wanting a piece of them, which boils down to their time and attention, can become draining when they don't have enough time for everyone who wants it. Jesus recognized the importance of preserving some sense of normalcy by withdrawing from all the acclaim and attention that the people were giving him. Luke 5:16 adds to this by revealing "But Jesus often withdrew to lonely places and prayed." I believe this is the key to sanity, a withdrawal from population. Go where others don't go. Go where we can't normally be reached. Get away to places where we can't be interrupted, places with solitude. He didn't retreat in surrender; he retreated to regroup and renew and then to return to his work. His strength was renewed by prayer. Celebrity that becomes notorious, victimizing - - read that as "destroyed by success" - - must seek spiritual strength. Verse 16 reveals, "Jesus often withdrew." When life is de-energizing us at an alarming rate, we need to re-energize at an increasing rate. The scripture states he "often withdrew to lonely places and prayed" which is significant as the principle spiritual exercise was quantity (often withdrew), and quality (to lonely places and prayed). It isn't just getting away that is important; it's also what we do when we get there. He prayed. The example for spiritual renewal has been set by the greatest celebrity who ever lived.

Mark 2:1-2, "A few days later, when Jesus again entered Capernaum, the people heard that he had come home. So many gathered that there was no room left, not even outside the door, and he preached to them." What do celebrities bring to people that they make a mad rush to be near them? In Jesus' case, the reality was he brought healing and hope, which is what the crowds wanted and anticipated. At that moment in time, the crowd was welcoming a home-grown hero, someone who went outside their community and made good on becoming a greater figure than local popularity. A hero's welcome back home, not just for doing well but becoming famous. Pretty much everyone wants a piece of the person who has gone beyond local notoriety.

Mark 2:13, "Once again Jesus went out beside the lake. A large crowd came to him, and he began to teach them." Some celebrities enjoy their fortune through specific venues, having as their outlet a place of familiarity. Jesus has no specific channel that he preferred to be seen in, nor distinct singular method that his popularity embraced. He was comfortable with crowds, small groups, and solitude. Large crowds came to him always, and unsolicited. There were no billboards, radio pronouncements, social media outreach, or print advertising to entice viewers, followers, or seekers. It was simply word-of-mouth exclamations of his deeds and actions, much akin to the wonders of someone's performance or their genius at captivating an audience's attention. Albeit in Jesus' situation it was miracles, teachings, and personality.

The pattern in his life was now to the point that everywhere he traveled, people by the multitude automatically wanted to be near him. Mark 3:7-10, "Jesus withdrew with his disciples to the lake, and a large crowd from Galilee followed. When they heard all, he was doing, many people came to him from Judea, Jerusalem, Idumea, and the regions across the Jordan and around Tyre and Sidon. Because of the crowd, he told his disciples to have a small boat ready for him to keep the people from crowding him. "For he had healed many, so that those with diseases were pushing forward to touch him." To be honest and fair about some celebrities, crowds become attracted to them for what they represent. People seek out celebrities for their presence because that presence brings to them something they believe they need or want. But celebrities also need distance sometimes, to keep from being "crowded," or to keep from being overwhelmed. Sometimes when lives are being touched, people want more and sanity, if not safety, must require precautions against the demands.

The Prime Pattern

Mark 3:13, "Jesus went up into the hills and called to him those he wanted, and they came to him." Luke 6:12 adds to that same event, "One of those days Jesus went out into the hills to pray and spent the night praying to God." Recuperation may take many forms, but in setting the example of rejuvenation of oneself for the rigors of celebrity, or for that matter the burden of life, it seems apparent that the prime pattern must be focused on spiritual renewal to God and maintaining a grounding in healthy relationships. Downtime and alone time, absent the crowds and the pace, should be exercised in a celebrity's life.

Matthew 8:1, "When Jesus came down from the mountainside, large crowds followed him." The crowds were already with him on the mountainside. They're with us when we're engaged in big things, or the things we have done, and they follow us for what we continue to do. At this time, Jesus had just finished the Beatitudes. How many celebrities have had a historic, defining moment that all will remember as a pinnacle of success, or some event that singles them out as brilliant, remarkable, and entrenches their celebrity even deeper? Mark 4:1, "On another occasion Jesus began to teach by the lake. The crowd that gathered around him was so large that he got into a boat and sat in it out on the lake, while all the people were along the shore at the water's edge." He kept doing the same thing, and they kept coming to the same thing. If people like the thing that a celebrity brings, they'll keep coming. Whatever attracts must keep happening for people to stay or come back. Not every celebrity can stay on top of their game. Some must reinvent themselves in order to keep the crowds; however, Jesus never changed. When he decided to be spontaneous, the throngs were in the wings. How many have the notoriety to fill seats on short notice?

Popular culture is known by trends and by those who are in that trend. Popular culture also has its leaders. With the constant ebb and flow of those in the lead, the "flavor of the month" varies. Celebrities has social circles of their own. The sports celebrities are known more to each other.

Entertainment celebrities have closer interaction with each other than they would, say, to business celebrities. The political celebrities have their cliques. Nonetheless, circles of celebrity's cross paths for several reasons. Jesus crossed paths with John the Baptist as celebrities would. In Luke 9:7-9 and Mark 6:14, we find that King Herod heard about Jesus, for his name had become well known, and he tried to find Jesus. Some celebrities seek out audiences with other celebrities to build alliances or to build their own status by affiliation with each other. Celebrity builds upon celebrity. Name recognition keeps the spotlight going. King Herod wanted to meet this famous person because "he was perplexed."

No Time To Eat

Then, because so many people were coming and going that they did not even have a chance to eat, he (Jesus) said to them, "Come with me by yourselves to a quiet place and get some rest." So they went away by themselves in a boat to a solitary place. But many who saw them leaving recognized them and ran on foot from all the towns and got there ahead of them.
Mark 6:31-33

This is indicative of the rabid fans of popular culture. We must tell the truth and acknowledge that there were blatant differences in why they rushed and crowded Jesus and the disciples, in that there were miracles taking place, the likes of which no one had ever seen in this consistent quantity. The dynamic of being sought after and mobbed by others who want to be with a celebrity, and those closest to a celebrity, are similar in principle especially the lengths that some will go to. They didn't even have time to eat! Consider the pace that was being kept by these public demands. When word gets out about where and when a celebrity arrives, the adoring crowds will be ahead of schedule to get a glimpse, an autograph, or to shake hands. No wonder many celebrities live in controlled environments and must take expensive security-laden vacations to remote or posh exclusive locations normally inaccessible to the general population. They go alone or with the typical entourage.

Matthew 15:30, "Great crowds came to him, bringing the lame, the blind, the crippled, the dumb and many others, and laid them at his feet, and he healed them." The truth here is that when you have something significant to offer, and the people are blessed by it, whether they need it or just want it, they will show up in droves. Be reminded, though, no one could offer what Jesus offered nor what he still does! Matthew 15:32, "Jesus called his disciples to him and said, 'I have compassion for these people; they have already been with me three days and have had nothing to eat. I do not want to send them away hungry.'" One of the hallmarks of a credible celebrity is an honest connection at a personal level to those who follow. This helps carry the devotion factor. When a celebrity identifies with their devotees, it keeps "the ties that bind."

Honest Inventory

Matthew 15:39 makes a telling point about timing. "After Jesus had sent the crowd away..." There comes a point when the autograph session must end, the lights should get turned out, and the celebrity needs to move on. There's nothing wrong with honestly and respectfully sending everyone home, especially the hangers-on. A celebrity must balance work, family, and the public with polite insistence. In Luke 9:18 Jesus asked the question, "Who do the crowds say that I am?" There's nothing wrong with a celebrity taking inventory of their status with those who follow them, if the people responsible for compiling the answers give honest feedback. An analysis of one's standing from an evaluation of public opinion can be useful as a reference for future endeavors. What do people think of me? How do I compare with others in my celebrity genre? Does the court of public opinion see me favorably? Does this bode well? Should my strategy change? Do I need to shake up staff? And the scrutiny continues.

Mark 9:14, "When they came to the other disciples, they (Jesus and three disciples) saw a large crowd around them." One simple lesson to be learned here is that people follow the people who follow, or are closely connected to, celebrity. From the words of Mark 9:30-31, "They left that place and passed through Galilee. Jesus did not want anyone to know where they were, because he was teaching his disciples," we learn that sometimes secrecy becomes crucial. Let only the "have-to-knows" know. Strategy-planning sessions, management focus, mentoring, future anticipations, and vision casting must be devoid of disruptions. "Hold the phone calls; this meeting is of highest importance." Sometimes distractions must be anticipated and eliminated so that a celebrity and their team can get together and focus on the future. Consider John 7:12 which informs, "Among the crowds there was widespread whispering about him. Some said, 'He is a good man,' others replied, 'No, he deceives the people.'" One thing every celebrity will undergo is controversy. At some point, someone will have something against them, maybe for good reason. There will be stories that are wrong on the facts, exaggerated on substance, and perhaps outright lies.

Celebrities have supporters and detractors; those who are for them, against them, and indifferent altogether. The tabloids, gossip columns, social media, and the general populace will have commentary on who they are and what they're all about. It's the interpretation or version of the celebrity's life that they believe, accurate or not. The signal character issue, especially from someone's detractors, is whether that celebrity is a hypocrite, particularly along the lines of the image they have created for themselves or become enveloped in, and then promote as quasi-reality. Once the truth comes out that the celebrity isn't true to their image, then contention arises. The reality needs to be that truthfulness and openness about oneself should be clear. When celebrities reveal themselves honestly and "let the chips fall where they may," at least they won't have anything to hide, perhaps nothing to apologize for, and they'll learn who's for them and against them, and why.

Jesus performed many miracles and had the greatest teachings that moved the crowds, which promoted his celebrity. Even with tremendous opposition, as in John 7:31, "Still, many in the crowd put their faith in him." This appears to be a big principle of why renown is established and maintained. The celebrity has accomplished or is doing something of significance. That's what attracts attention. People who are affected in some way by those accomplishments or deeds are the supporters, followers, if not even beneficiaries. John 8:2 states, "At dawn he appeared again in the temple courts, where all the people gathered around him, and he sat down to teach them." The thing that also keeps fame going is the celebrity's proficiency and consistency. They must be good at what they're doing, and for the most part, they must keep doing it; otherwise, the celebrity can fall into the used-to-be, has-been, washed-up group...the "one-hit wonders" and someone's "fifteen seconds of fame." Jesus never lost his edge. Obviously, star athletes could transition from their youthful athletic prowess to become a commentator or coaching celebrity, still maintaining public connection with what got them there. Singers or dancers, who can no longer perform at prior levels, could move forward gracefully as mentors. The specific transition may no longer have direct involvement but would have definite contributions that maintain the celebrity image.

Who Is In The Crowd?

Luke 12:1 informs us that a crowd of many thousands had gathered, and they were trampling on one another. Some would "give their right arm" to have this kind of attention and adoration. Be reminded, there can be basically two kinds of crowds; the vicarious crowd that wants to live life through the celebrity, and the desperate crowd looking for someone to supply answers for their needs. This was a desperate crowd, as most of Jesus' were. Luke 13:22, "Then Jesus went through the towns and villages, teaching as he made his way to Jerusalem." People didn't just come to Christ; he also went to them. He brought his gifts and talents to those who hadn't been exposed to what he had to offer. He kept building his ministry and attracting others. Celebrities shouldn't pull back from smaller venues, which are opportunities to find that personal connection that may be missing from the large-crowd dynamic. The travel game is one which politicians, athletes, and entertainers know so well.

Luke 15:1 reveals a telling point, "Now many tax collectors and 'sinners' were gathering around to hear him." Not everyone who aspires to public recognition will find mass appeal. In Christ's case, he had mass appeal, and a special appeal for a niche group, the tax collectors and "sinners." Jesus basically did two things -- He did miracles and he taught. Most celebrities do only one or two things well. Even if they transition, they may leave something behind, but a celebrity usually starts out with a niche market, or appeal. Even when they transcend localized fame, a celebrity is usually accomplished in just a few things. "Make the best of what you got." See who and what it attracts and then go from there. Embrace the niche you are blessed with.

Jesus' celebrity continued in Matthew 19:2, large crowds followed him. In Mark 10:13 people were bringing little children to Jesus to have him touch them. Mark 10:46 states in part, "As Jesus and his disciples, together with a large crowd, were leaving the city..." One of my takes on the "little children incident," as it also concerns celebrity, is that care must be taken to nurture the next generation of followers. Spend time investing in the people for the future. The next age group needs connection, especially in the church.

John 12:9, "Meanwhile a large crowd of Jews found out that Jesus was there and came, not only because of him, but also to see Lazarus, whom he had raised from the dead." Who wouldn't want to see that? Celebrity is known for its (imaginative) exploits, and those who are advantaged by it. Some celebrities have people around them who are connected to them by association, partnership, or teaming. When one's name is mentioned, another name may be associated. A select few people bring name recognition to others' celebrity when their own name is talked about. Matthew 21:8-9 and Mark 11:8-9 reveal that, in the process of his triumphal entry, a very large crowd spread their cloaks and branches on the road before him and joyfully shouted his praises. It's endearing to celebrities to feel appreciated, to have the favor of the crowd, and the gifts they bring. Jesus was not put back by the crowd's praises; if anyone had earned the love and respect of multitudes, it would have been him. In earnest, many a celebrity wants a response like this. The standing ovations, the fan clubs, the social media attention, the must-read articles about their every move and their next work. Most celebrities want the talk, the attention, and the awareness. Handling it with maturity, balance, respect, and humility can make the difference in the celebrity's greatness and longevity.

(Dis)Connection

There is a lesson in Mark 11:18, Matthew 21:46, and

in Mark 14:2 about celebrity protection. When certain leaders decided they wanted to kill Jesus, they were afraid of him because of the esteem in which the whole crowd held him. When someone has mass appeal, or even a niche audience, and others come against them, the fans afford a level of scrutiny or backlash that the normal citizen doesn't experience. The followers may write letters, boycott, picket, unsubscribe, unfollow or block, withhold support from the critics, vote against them, or use whatever means at their disposal to show disapproval of the actions against their celebrity. Consideration must be given in taking on celebrities. Of course, celebrity wars have been known to break out against each other. That makes for interesting stories and pop culture competition. Mark 12:37, "The large crowd listened to him with delight." Part of the appeal of celebrities is the contribution they give to their followers. Jesus always gave his fullest. Celebrities would be well reminded to use their talents, gifts, and abilities to the utmost for their intended audience, hopefully for the glory of God, and to make a positive difference in the world, like Christ.

All four Gospels record that as Jesus was speaking in the Garden of Gethsemane, Judas arrived with a large crowd armed with swords and clubs. They had been sent by the leadership of those who opposed him. In most celebrities' lives, especially the enduring ones, they not only find people against them, but might see themselves become an object of direct confrontation. Opposition sometimes isn't content to win out in the arena of ideas or simple public affection but may bring outright rivalry to a celebrity's doorstep. Friendly, aggressive competition may shift into hostile antagonism, alter into character assassination, and morph to career (celebrity) destruction. The negative publicity about a celebrity, that descends to debilitating propaganda, can spiral out of control until there is no recovery, especially when public opinion is against them. Sometimes the attacks happen behind the scenes, in the shadows, taking advantage of vulnerable moments to strike. A celebrity can become isolated, marginalized, discredited, and abandoned. At some point, the public is involved in this devolution, to sustain the momentum brought by the detractors.

Luke 23:1, "Then the whole assembly rose and led him (Jesus) off to Pilate." Opposition to someone's celebrity will come from every direction, from those within their genre, category, field, and from those against it to begin with. From those who want to take the celebrity's place, position, or power, and from those who think it shouldn't have existed to begin with. Every group has special interests or niche groupings within its own ranks; each clamoring, clawing, and climbing to have their agenda maintained and/or promoted. The politics of destruction has no boundaries. At some point, celebrities may have their career cut short; not because their star has burned out, or they're past their prime, or even because the general public has had enough, but simply because of career assassination. After the crowd has been persuaded from whatever source (Matthew 27:20 and Mark 15:11) to be against the celebrity, inevitable loss will occur. The celebrity becomes a casualty in the struggle for dominance. Matthew 27:17, "So when the crowd had gathered..." This turn of events became a public issue and the voice of public opinion had turned; unanimously, they chose Barabbas over Jesus.

Well-liked, admired celebrities can also become notorious or infamous for transgressions they make resulting in the expected and conspicuous loss of respect, support, and acceptance they previously enjoyed. Christ knows what it's like to be ordinary, then to become synonymous with achievement, and then to fall unceremoniously out of favor in a short period of time. How he handled the crowds, dealt with his inner circle, and maintained stability can give every celebrity pause for reflection on these principles.

Not everything that can be said about the question "Does God really understand celebrity?" has been brought forth here, but enough to prove that the answer is emphatically "yes!"

Chapter 8

The BIRD:
Betrayal, Injustice, Rejection, Desertion

Betrayal, Injustice, Rejection, Desertion - - these words and their definitions are related to one another. Every betrayal is an injustice. Every desertion has some type of rejection attached to it. Their meanings typically do not stand alone when we are talking about interpersonal relationships. As opposed to you may reject a specific flavor of ice cream and it affects no one in the normal scope of things. Throughout this chapter, these words and their meanings will be used together and at times somewhat interchangeably, hence the acronym of The BIRD. Was this a play on words? Yes, it was by design. But let's get past that issue and get into the heart of "Does God understand getting The BIRD.?" Does God understand betrayal, injustice, rejection, and desertion, even if they're all mixed?

We generally give more value to someone's credibility and reputation when that person's experience(s) match ours. Remember that according to God's viewpoint, he "lowered himself" (Philippians 2:6-8). In Hebrews 2:7, 9, God reminds us that Christ was made a little lower than the Angels for a while. We established before that God became a human, took on our life's experiences, and went through what we went through, if not literally at least in principle. He got down to our level; he got into our everyday existence. He lived a life as we do. God has the "street cred." He doesn't just have the "ivory tower" education of sitting on Heaven's throne, saying "I know what you're going through," while never having gone through it. God isn't piously mouthing off something intellectual; he's empathizing experientially. God understands these things directly.

Who Is In What Together?

What are some things you've gone through with others? Married folk have gone through things as a couple. Siblings and relatives can say they've experienced things as family. Doctors and patients can say they've gone through health issues together. People at work can point to getting through work issues together, issues that the spouse, relatives, and doctor usually haven't participated in. We go through things together in different groupings or, as I explained before, with different identities of we or us. That implies "togetherness." The phrase is warranted - - "We're in this together" and there are different interlocking circles of togetherness, or even a matrix of togetherness, but what happens when the circle/matrix of togetherness ends? Not because a project ends and we're done working together, not because I've moved and some relationships no longer have their heightened dynamic, but because of The BIRD.

In Matthew 26:21, Jesus is in the upper room with the disciples. "And while they were eating, he said, 'I tell you the truth, one of you will betray me.'" A prophetic announcement of what was about to happen and a generic prediction of who would betray him. How does it play out in your mind when you know the person who is about to do something wrong, or is in the process, you are the victim, and the consequences are going to be horrific? In Matthew 26:25, Jesus informs Judas that he knows he is the one who is about to perform the "dastardly deed." Jesus also warns in the gospels "Woe to the man who betrays him," and that it would have been "better if he had never been born" (Mark 14:21). In John 13:26-30, we find that Judas goes out immediately after communion to complete his betrayal, to fulfill the evil intent in his heart.

What was it that broke Judas' circle of togetherness with Jesus and, for that matter, the other disciples? What darkness comes over some that, after going through things, they break ranks, they break bonds, they betray trust, and go a different path? What was Judas' issue(s)? Let's first look at the togetherness of this group. Judas was chosen to be in the inner circle. When the disciples were given small group teachings, he was there. When they were given power to exorcise demons, he was one of them. Mark 3:16-19 details the appointing of the disciples, of which Judas was one, and in Matthew 10:5-10, we read of the sending out of the twelve disciples to do miracles, which included Judas. He was there when Jesus walked on water, opened the eyes of the blind, healed the crippled, raised the dead, healed leprosy, multiplied little amounts of food and fed the thousands. He was part of the beginning of Christianity! After all he had seen, experienced, and participated in, why would he walk away? What was his motive, and what was the hang-up?

Matthew 26:6-13, Mark 14:3-9, and John 12:2-8 relate the incident of a woman named Mary pouring about a pint of an expensive perfume from an alabaster jar onto Jesus' feet and head. Some of the disciples became angry at the perceived waste. Their argument was that the perfume could have been sold and the money given to the poor. Jesus defended the act as preparation for his upcoming burial which would mean his impending death. Jesus said in John 12:8 that they would always have the poor with them, but not always have him. Then in John 12:6, we are clued into Judas' real motive. It reads that "he did not say this because he cared about the poor, but because he was a thief; as keeper of the money bag, he used to help himself to what was put into it." It was at that point that Judas went to the chief priests and the officers of the temple guard to discuss with them how he would betray Jesus for thirty silver coins. After an action plan was developed and agreed upon, he waited for his opportunity, as related in Matthew 26:14-16, Mark 14:10-11, and Luke 22:3-6.

Betrayal

There we find some serious clues as to Judas' betrayal motives. It appears as if he comes to the rationalization that the money train is coming to an end because Jesus is going to die soon; all the donations would dry up and his "hand in the cookie jar" time was ending. He cast his lot in with the bad guys, hoping to curry favor with them by ending his affiliation with Jesus and the other disciples. His thinking follows thus -- "If Jesus' time is short-lived, let's just get it over with by betrayal...I'll have ingratiated myself with the rulers who'll still be here, and I'll get by with their largesse." Judas was already a betrayer before his one-on-one betrayal of Jesus. As a thief who helped himself to the money bag of the poor, he betrayed all the people who donated money in good faith that it would be handled with integrity. He betrayed the other disciples who may have depended on some of the proceeds for necessary living expenses. He betrayed the trust that leadership (Jesus) placed in him to be a trustworthy soul. Finally, he betrayed the very poor he pretended to care so much about. His money-grubbing ways were exposed in Matthew 26:15 when he asked, "What are you willing to give me (pay me) if I hand him over to you?" (Read "betray him"). The fact that Judas sought them out for that opportunity was especially egregious; no one had approached him or was blackmailing him.

It seems his false sense of preservation took precedence over any sense of loyalty. It's not like he switched careers and went to another company. What kind of character is it who, when the people in the circle or matrix of togetherness are counting on them, purposely disposes of their loyalty? Judas waited for his moment. After the Last Supper, he left to complete his betrayal. While Jesus was saying prayers in the Garden of Gethsemane, Judas went to the chief priests and elders of the people, gave them insider information of Jesus' location, and returned with a large, armed crowd.

Judas also arranged to identify Jesus by greeting him with a kiss (Matthew 26:47-56, Mark 14:43-50, Luke 22:47-53 and John 18:2-12). A kiss was a customary Middle Eastern greeting still employed today. The Bible encourages us to greet one another with a holy kiss (2 Corinthians 13:12). When Judas called Jesus "Rabbi," which means Teacher, and kissed him, it was supposed to be a sign of respect. Hence the question Jesus asked in Luke 22:48, "Judas, are you betraying the son of man with a kiss?" Basically, this was an incredulous act. How "low can you go" that you not only are a traitor, but you betray with a symbolic gesture of love and respect? The aghast would say, "How could you do this?" Although some would point out that Judas was later seized with remorse when he realized the consequences of his actions (Matthew 27:3-10), that doesn't change his ultimate responsibility in this. It was his betrayal that set the "wheels in motion" leading to the crucifixion.

Be reminded, Judas' involvement wasn't a slip of the tongue, or a momentary lack of judgment; this was premeditated, purposeful and arranged. People are betrayed and victimized by traitors in various fashion, whether it's the military as "Benedict Arnolds," corporate secrets, client privileges violated, or adultery (a whole chapter section on that one). Betrayal goes so deep and cuts so hard that some people's names are synonymous with it. Again, "Benedict Arnold." Does "Et tu, Brute" ring a bell? Similarly, Judas is identified as a "snake in the grass," someone lying in wait to do harm, an untrustworthy soul. Take onto account that it's not betrayal if it's not a friend, a confidant, or someone in the circle of togetherness. An enemy can't betray you; that's why they're an enemy, they're already against you. When you think someone is with you and then they go "all Judas on you," that's what cuts the deepest. Every betrayal, at some level, includes an injustice of some sort.

Injustice

In Chapter Two, on the death of a loved one, I explain somewhat the injustice of what Jesus endured after his betrayal at the hands of the Jewish leadership, as it concerns their being vanguards of the religion. I am now going to put greater emphasis on the account. In Matthew 26 and Mark 14, the story unfolds that the chief priests and the whole Sanhedrin (the religious teaching body of the Jews) came together to look for false evidence against Jesus so they could put him to death. Disreputable fellows testified but their statements didn't agree. Even some spurious charges, that didn't quite line up about Jesus tearing down and rebuilding the temple, arose. Finally, the high priest put the "thousand-dollar question" to Jesus and asked him if he is the Christ, the Son of God, to which Jesus affirmed in Matthew 26:64, "Yes, it is as you say." This was the confession "straw that broke the camel's back." They accused him of blasphemy, which was punishable by death, but when you examine the record of the conspiracy, you see it was out of fear. Read Mark 11:15-18 in which Jesus cleared the moneychangers from the temple, and the chief priests and teachers of the law began looking for a way to kill him. Basically, because the whole crowd was being persuaded by him, they feared the competition. Some will resort to character assassination, conspiracy, and collusion in order to maintain the status quo and resist any quest for freedom from all versions of sin, including their own. Note the story of Jesus Is Lord of the Sabbath told in Matthew 12:1-14 in which he exposes their hypocrisy in creating laws that they themselves would not obey if it suited their personal interests, let alone the violation of "Thou shall not murder, bear false witness, covet, etc."

When the Jewish leaders appeared before Pilate, as told in John 18:31, they admitted they had no right to execute anyone. Yet they were determined to lie and press forward with politics to Pilate and Herod in order to fulfill their murderous ambitions against an innocent man. Pilate's wife warned him about a troubling dream she had, that Jesus was innocent (Matthew 27:19). Her warning included to not have anything to do with this mess. For Pilate to "steer clear" of their drama. Pilate informed the leaders that neither he nor Herod found any basis for the death penalty (Luke 23:13-16). The crowd became riotous, and Pilate tried to placate them with a cursory beating of Jesus instead of crucifixion, since there wasn't any justification for it (Luke 23:16-22). The crowd did, in Luke 23:23, what professional political agitators still do today when they seek injustice against someone for ulterior motives, when they don't have the truth on their side; just scream louder until they wear down those who stand in their way.

Pilate knew their motives. Matthew 27:18 informs that Pilate knew it was out of envy that the leaders had handed Jesus over to him to be crucified. They were jealous of Jesus' popularity and the way that the people were persuaded by him. They didn't want to lose their power, so they tried to do character assassinations with trick questions and found that he had answers the people enjoyed and accepted. This infuriated them because their manmade, legalistic, mumbo-jumbo laws were keeping people down and out, which they reveled in because it gave them even greater power over people's lives. Jesus came along and the "apple cart" started to get upset. The people were learning that they didn't need the existing power structure any longer and that they could have a life of freedom from it. The rulers had their turning point against Jesus and found a co-conspirator in Judas who, in the dark of night, helped them arrest Jesus, file false charges against him without public scrutiny, propose the death penalty from a "kangaroo court," and have it enforced by the public officials who had the power to really make their problem go away with crucifixion. When the government exonerated him and couldn't justify the death penalty, they shouted all the louder, stirred up the people who didn't know the truth, falsely accusing Pilate of being no friend of Caesar's (John 19:12), thus threatening his status and political standing. Until finally, amid all the commotion, they wore Pilate down and he gave in to the injustice, knowing full well it was wrong. There is "nothing new under the sun" (Ecclesiastes 1:9).

Many people see injustice and try to do something about it, yet life still moves forward with victims of injustice at the personal level, at the local community level, and at the national and international levels. Look at the false witnesses, the false accusations, the trumped-up charges, the mistreatment, and most importantly, the ultimate penalty. This wasn't a zoning issue that didn't go the people's way. The recovery from many injustices is typically a short period of feeling gruff and angry and then we move on, but there was no turning back from this situation. An injustice that can't be rectified, or at least recovered from in some fashion, is the worst kind. All of us can think of spectacularly unfair things that have happened to others. We all have witnessed those in authority positions engaging without truthfulness in questionable practices and shenanigans that unduly benefit them, and when it hits at the awful expense of others, especially the vulnerable among us, the disgust factor kicks into overdrive. Whenever you're in the throes of some type of reckoning, and you believe that justice has not prevailed, just remember that God himself was a victim.

God has been lied about, faced false charges, faced the death penalty, and had the greatest injustices brought against him. All those injustices were preceded by rejection.

Rejection

God had to face rejection at different times in various areas. Rejection of his teachings, such as when Jesus spoke about his being the Bread of Life (John 6:25) and John 6:66 concludes, "From this time many of his disciples turned back and no longer followed him." There are examples of the rejection of his being the Christ or Deity, rejection of his personhood or his character, and finally, rejection of his life. We can and do face rejection of many things in our lives. Some we barely notice; others are terrible wounding's. Some rejections that come our way we will never understand and some rejections we should try to learn from.

When Can Rejection Be A Good Thing?

Rejection can be a good thing if we're willing to learn the lesson it offers. It can add to our personal growth and help us improve our lives. Such as: We are rejected for a position we applied for because we lack the necessary skill set or education. If we are willing to take the time and expense of adding that skill set or getting that education, because the position is something we really want, then the rejection was a favor; otherwise, we might have been "in over our head" and failed miserably, which contributes nothing overall and could have been a greater embarrassment than not getting the position or promotion.

Maybe we were one of the last to be picked for playing sports. In all honesty, usually it's because the physical talent we possess doesn't contribute to the team's success. If we're a star player, chances are we'll be selected even if we're not well liked. Our options, otherwise, are to build up our ability the best we can and keep trying, or just make the best of it. If we don't want to improve in that area, the rejection of being picked last doesn't mean that much.

Perhaps we're being rejected as a potential or existing

boyfriend or girlfriend. What's the reason for the rejection? Is it because the rejecter believes that someone better has or will come along? For that matter, why would we want to be in a relationship where we're always second-guessing the other person's contentment status? Or perhaps it's because we didn't present ourselves as a viable candidate for another's affections? Maybe we need to put on some deodorant, brush our teeth, and pull up our pants? Just asking...is the rejection an indication that legitimate improvements are needed?

Maybe my offer on a house was rejected because someone else put in a higher offer. My application for a scholarship was rejected because I didn't apply myself academically enough in high school and other candidates beat me out. The food I put on the table was rejected because I forgot some ingredients and it tasted awful. My ideas were rejected at the staff meeting because they were not well thought out, and my plans were poorly designed. Some rejections are learning and personal growth opportunities.

When Rejection Isn't a Good Thing

Even when rejection isn't a good thing, we can always learn from it. The flip side to the self-improvement revelations...is the real reason I didn't get the promotion because the other person played office politics and schmoozed with the bosses at golf games? Is the reason

I didn't get the girl/guy was because they were superficial and wanted to play games with people's lives? Was my scholarship not advanced because someone else knew someone who forwarded the applications to people with connections? There are reasons that are valid for rejection and there are reasons which, if not suspect, are downright wrong. If anything, Christ knows what it is to be rejected.

We find God's confession of this reality in 1 Samuel 8:6-8, when the people demanded a king, and God tells the prophet Samuel that they were rejecting him (God) as their king, and that it was the people's pattern. Isaiah 53:3, "He was despised and rejected by men." This was prophetic of Christ in that there would come a time in his life that mankind would reject him and everything he represented. John 1:11, "He came to that which was his own, but his own did not receive him." The enlightenment we have is that God humbled himself by becoming a human, walked among us physically and literally, was despised and rejected by those he came to help, and was then murdered for his efforts. That kind of rejection had to hurt. Christ came to help us then and is still ready to help us now. Unfortunately, the bulk of people then and now are still rejecting Christ.

In John 18:28-40, Pilate spoke to Jesus about the situation they were in, the tumult over his innocence, and the Jews wanting him crucified. In verse 35, Pilate stated, "It was your people and your chief priests who handed you over to me." Pilate acknowledged the rejection of Jesus by those who were his own yet were not receiving him, and by those who were despising him and rejecting him. We all have faced rejection of some nature and to varying degrees. Perhaps the worst type is when our own people are rejecting us. Jesus had to face this constantly from the leadership that resisted him, but now the people had gone against him.

Jesus had to face this when in Mark 3:21 his family went to take charge of him, for they said, "He is out of his mind." There is more on this in another chapter, but God knows what it's like to face rejection in one's family. Many know the story of Job. A whole book of the Bible is dedicated to his story. In essence, Job was a man who had everything. He had great wealth with a multitude of livestock and servants, lots of kids who seemed to be one big happy family, a great reputation, and he apparently enjoyed good personal health. In short order he lost it all. While suffering, he seemed to have lost the support of his wife. Job had three friends who came along to show their support: Eliphaz, Bildad, and Zophar. A lot has been said about what went wrong with their visit with Job, mainly how they got it wrong about the reasons for his suffering. The one thing—at least in motive, and to start with in practice—was the bond they had with him. Job had everything taken from him and they came to comfort him. It didn't go as it should have but, to give credit where credit is due, how many people would go to the lengths they did to go and sympathize with him and comfort him? Eliphaz, Bildad, and Zophar traveled together to go to Job, then sat with him for seven days and didn't say a word (Job 2:11-13). Their presence alone spoke volumes about their commitment to the friendship they shared.

How many would take a week's vacation from their lives to help someone else? Would we weep aloud? Would we sit silently for seven days and nights and feel another's pain? The one thing they didn't do was abandon him, or desert him, in his time of need. This is akin to sitting in a hospital somewhere, lending the unspoken support that others may need, being in it together. Revisiting John 6:66, "From this time many of his disciples turned back and no longer followed him," we understand that the rejection always comes before the desertion, the abandonment. In some cases, as with Judas, it comes before the betrayal. How many soldiers desert their army, which is to really to be deserting the country it represents, because they no longer believe in its ideals or causes? This is what happened to Jesus -- some disciples no longer believed in what they were following, so they rejected and deserted him.

Desertion

Tragically, many children and mates are abandoned by a parent or spouse who is supposed to be committed to the relationship. This family dysfunction has too many facets to deal with in this book but, suffice to say, most family desertions are not because of some political or philosophical disagreements, rather are simply matters of selfishness and personal sin.

Obviously, there are times when we must abandon a "sinking ship." How long do we stay with an employer whose business is "going down the tubes" before we start looking for another job? We're not deserting the employer if we're trying to maintain support for our family and household. Jesus predicted that his closest supporters would desert him. In Matthew 26:31 he said to his disciples, "This very night you will all fall away on account of me." Peter responded in verse 33 that "Even if all fall away on account of you, I never will." Jesus then prophesied that Peter would disown him three times before the rooster crowed. In verse 35, Peter declared, "Even if I have to die with you, I will never disown you" (The BIRD; betrayal, injustice, rejection and desertion) and all the other disciples said the same.

One of the valid criticisms of Peter, is his insistence of loyalty, followed a few hours later by his denial of Christ. It's only fair to point out that all the other disciples felt, said, and declared the same fealty as Peter did. Let's examine how this played out. As Jesus was arrested, scripture reveals in Matthew 26:56 that all the disciples fled. Did the disciples see the fledgling movement as that proverbial sinking ship because the leader was now in custody? In

Matthew 26:74-75, after being confronted three times about being a follower of Jesus, Peter began to curse and denied Christ the third time by saying, "I don't know the man!" At that point the rooster crowed, and Peter went outside and wept bitterly because he was reminded of the words Jesus had spoken about his impending betrayal, the injustice of desertion, abandonment, and rejection (The BIRD). Understand that as abject failure, even though Peter was later reconciled to Christ.

After the disciples declared their commitment to Jesus to the point of death, Jesus found himself alone; Betrayed, the injustice of abandonment by those who swore allegiance, rejected by the disciples, and deserted by those who stood proud and tall with him at one time (The BIRD). Now Jesus was left to face things on his own. How many people have made expressions of devotion to a marriage, to a business endeavor, to parenting, and then were disloyal to those counting on their fidelity? What of the ones anticipating that reliability? The letdown factor is magnified, not just by the personal interest involved, but also by the repercussions or the aftermath of desertion.

There is another area of desertion, or at least the feeling of desertion, that I would like to consider. Mark 15:34 states, "And at the ninth hour (while on the cross) Jesus cried out in a loud voice, 'Eloi, Eloi, lama sabachthani?' – which means, 'My God, my God, why have you forsaken me?'" Many theologians believe that at some point, on the cross during his suffering, Christ took on the sin of the world and at that moment (2 Corinthians 5:21) "God made him who had no sin to be sin for us." The Father could not look upon his own son because of all the sin that was on him. Jesus felt God turning away from him and made the exclamation of being forsaken or deserted. Forgive me for what some would say is an oversimplification, but this isn't the venue to debate whether God deserted him or if Jesus simply felt that way. My purpose is to show that no matter what, Christ felt abandoned by God, and most agree that the sin of the world that had come upon him was the determining factor in his outlook. This leads us to probe the matter of why some sense a desertion from God. Should we not consider the implication that possibly there are sin issues in our lives that are bringing about feelings of desertion from God, or can I suggest, separation anxiety between us? A distancing caused by us and the resulting feelings.

This was the core of what Christ was going through. Sin had come upon him, and he was feeling the effects of it in his spirit. The "nitty-gritty" is that sin can interfere with our relationship with God. I stand by the reality that God never stops loving us, but unconditional love is not unconditional approval! If something in our lives is honestly displeasing to others, can we not feel another's disapproval in our spirit? The desertion that Christ was feeling from God was confirmation that something had come between them. Do we have those impressions at times? An honest soul would feel the distance, make confession to God, evaluate their lives, and move forward with any necessary changes they had to make in order to get back the perspective of "All is well with my soul" (Psalm 42:7). Sometimes, and I mean sometimes, the reason we're feeling separated from God, or forsaken, is because we are living our lives, engaging in activities, or exhibiting behavior that is against God's direction for us. Change in us would be the prescription for the healing of the relationship.

What To Do When You Get The BIRD

When you've experienced betrayal, injustice, rejection, and desertion (The BIRD), remind yourself that Christ did also, and if there's anyone who can understand what you're going through, it is he. Recovering from those wounds can take a long time and it may weaken us mentally, emotionally, and spiritually. To be rejected unfairly is to be treated as unworthy of consideration. When you've been cast aside as worthless, when you've been disgraced as contemptible, or when you have been shamed by degrading, despicable acts, remember that God also has experienced it too. He will comfort you from his own experiences, while being supportive of your recovery, thoughtful and caring toward your condition, and always with your best interest in mind. God has gotten The BIRD and he moved on. Praise the Lord!!

Chapter 9

The Omni-Experience Of God

Let's consider the Omniscience of God. The fact that God knows the facts. He knows the who, what, where when and how of something and someone. He also knows the why of things and the motives of people. Many people think that they are really in tune with who they are. Others may say that they don't know who they are, that they need to find themselves. I wonder if those people who need to find themselves, when they do, shake their own hands when they meet themselves for the first time. The facts are that God knows us better than anyone else, including ourselves. Look at all the people who know us, especially in the different roles or functions in life that we represent, whether for a moment or a lifetime. Yet God knows us better than anyone.

He Knows "The Why"

He knows the "why" of us. Why we do what we do. Why we don't do what we don't do. Why we say the things that we say, and why we don't say the things we don't say. He knows the why of our dreams, ambitions, and aspirations. He knows the why of our disappointments, frustrations, and longings. He knows the why of our doing good and the why of when we do bad, even when we don't admit it to ourselves. Sometimes we sear our conscience to the truth of what we've done, or what we're thinking, or even what we're going through. Sometimes we don't admit the truth to ourselves. How many times has someone asked, "How are you doing?" and we automatically respond, "Just great," when perhaps, in truthfulness, our life is falling apart? There is a reference-point reality that needs illuminating here; our reference point is that, in the big picture of things, we have salvation in Christ, therefore, we're doing great. But if our reference point is day-to-day survival, then the unspoken thought is that the culture expects us to respond in the positive, potentially leading us to lie, when all we want to do is scream because of the hurt and pain. Does the checkout clerk really care when they ask, "How are you doing?" Maybe, but not likely. It's just a polite (or even company-required) expression for "hello," not meant to elicit any truthful dialogue, but to encourage the continuing exchange and to set us in a friendly environment. How many times do people walk past us down the street or hallway and ask, "How are you doing?" and keep walking, hardly acknowledging any reply we give? Some of us are a little bit more truthful and don't answer with "I'm doing great," instead, we may say," I'm hanging in there." We generally do know what we're going through, and why, and maybe a few others, for whatever reasons, also understand. Remember, God knows everything about us, including the why. He knows why we're going through what we're going through.

The Omnipresence of God reveals that God is everywhere with us. That's certainly a humbling thought when we're in the bathroom, or when we're having that argument about nothing with a loved one, or when we're involved in intimate encounters. God's presence is everywhere, at the same time. Jeremiah 23:23-24, "'Am I only a God nearby,' declares the Lord, 'and not a God far away? Can anyone hide in secret places so that I cannot see him?' declares the Lord. 'Do not I fill heaven and earth?' declares the Lord."

God's presence is witness to our lives, adding to everything he knows about us. Now this is the juncture to make distinctions among God's Omniscience, his all-knowingness, and God's Omnipresence, his all-presence, and God's Omni-experience, his all-experiencing attribute. God doesn't just experience our lives with us, but because he's in us, he experiences our lives as we do. He goes through what we go through. God's omnipresence can be said as "God with us." Matthew 28:20, "...and teaching them to obey everything I have commanded you. And surely, I am with you always, to the very end of the age." He is with us always; he will never leave us or forsake us.

> *If you love me, you will obey what I command. And I will ask the Father, and he will give you another counselor to be with you forever — the Spirit of truth. The world cannot accept him because it neither sees him nor knows him. But you know him, for he lives with you and will be in you.*
> John 14:15-17

> *You, however, are controlled not by the sinful nature, but by the Spirit, if the Spirit of God lives in you. And if anyone does not have the Spirit of Christ, he does not belong to Christ. But if Christ is in you, your body is dead because of sin, yet your spirit is alive because of righteousness. And if the Spirit of him who raised Jesus from the dead is living in you, he who raised Christ from the dead will also give life to your mortal bodies through his Spirit who lives in you.*
> Romans 8:9-11

Experiencing Our Lives

As a human, God personally experienced his own life; as God in us, he personally experiences our lives as well. I will detail later how this is, but there is one disclaimer:

God experiences everything we do except one thing - - he cannot and will not actively participate or engage in our sin. God does not lead us into sin. That would be to take us where he doesn't want to go or want us to go. He will allow us to be tempted, but not beyond what we can tolerate. 1 Corinthians 10:13, "No temptation has seized you except what is common to man. And God is faithful, he will not let you be tempted beyond what you can bear. But when you are tempted, he will also provide a way out so that you can stand up under it."

We all know the excuse-makers, but that scripture is an excuse-breaker. Humans are excuse-making machines for our trespasses. Adam blamed Eve and God, Eve blamed the serpent, and we've been blaming others ever since for the wrong things we do. Genesis Chapter 3 describes the situation. Some of the lines can be paraphrased like this: "We're only human; we just couldn't resist." Yes, we could have, we just didn't, or didn't resist enough. "We just had to give in." Really? God will not let us be tempted beyond our limitations, but we are typically led away by our own desires, passions, agendas, etc. James 1:14, "But each one is tempted when by his own evil desires, he is dragged away and enticed." Not only will God not let us be tempted past our capabilities to withstand, but he also doesn't want us to put ourselves unnecessarily into a position of temptation to begin with. Job 31:1, "I made a covenant with my eyes not to look lustfully at a girl." Job was avoiding the starting point.

The Risk Of Exposure

Psalm 1:1, "Blessed is the man who does not walk in the counsel of the wicked, or stand in the way of sinners, or sit in the seat of mockers." There are some exposures, activities, involvements that God wants us to avoid or have limits around. When we expose our bodies to some things, we risk becoming infected with whatever contagions exist. Engaging in some activities can lead to hepatitis, AIDS, colds, etc. Becoming exposed to certain high-risk factors can lead to illnesses, addictions, and diseases. We should take precautions in limiting our exposure to things that can lead to these results.

The same holds true for spiritual pollution and contagions. All sin is contagious in some manner or another. If we're around angry people all the time, we'll probably end up angrier. If we're exposed to impatient people excessively, we may become more impatient. It depends somewhat on our spiritual immune system. Different people have different spiritual immune systems or resistances. We should, and God wants us to, avoid the exposure to begin with, considering our own spiritual limitations and weaknesses. Recognize that we are "in the world but not of it" (John 15:19 and John 17:14-16), we must go to work, school, and have social interaction. Yet we must be careful of how intimate our engagements are. As a cultural saying goes about our physical health, "Garbage in, garbage out." So, the same for our spiritual health.

No one can deny that there are things on the internet, television, magazines, etc., that would be a contagion to our souls. Some would argue, "Well, it's there, what can we do about it?" Just as I don't need to eat rat poison to know that it's no good for me, there are many things that we should avoid which brings up the thought, "What does God personally experience when Christian's sin, since he is experiencing our lives as we are?" I would imagine disappointment, frustration, anger, hurt, and perhaps a sense of loss. Ephesians 4:30, "And do not grieve the Holy Spirit of God with whom you were sealed for the day of redemption."

I Thessalonians 5:19, "Do not put out the spirit's fire." Where is the spirit's fire? In us! God is warning us to not put out the fire of the Holy Spirit that is in us. For starters, God is telling us to not do something. It means we have the capability of doing what he doesn't want us to do. "Thou shalt not murder" (Exodus 20:13, Deuteronomy 5:17), and yet people do. "Thou shalt not commit adultery" (Exodus 20:14), yet people also do that. God warns us to not engage in sinful behaviors that we are capable of, because it's harmful to us as individuals and to society and thus quenching, or putting out, the fire of the Holy Spirit in us. The admonition is to avoid every kind of evil. Why? One reason is that if we don't, we start to embrace sin which could have the net effect of putting out the spirit's fire. Now that starts to affect the Shekinah (the glory of the divine presence as light; the invisible Glory of God) in us.

We can minimally dampen, or even put out, the evidence of the Spirit's fire at work in our lives by distancing ourselves from that fire. Yes, we can grieve God. Ephesians 4:31, "Get rid of all bitterness, rage, and anger, brawling and slander, along with every form of malice." One reason is that it makes for a bad example to others, but another reason is that these types of behaviors grieve the Holy Spirit and start to create a distance between us and God which, if left uncorrected, leads to quenching his fire. Ephesians 5:3, "But among you there must not be even a hint of sexual immorality, or of any kind of impurity, or of greed, because these are improper for God's holy people." Where is he? In us. Where do all these things originate? In us.

Creating Distance

What does it mean to profane? The typical answers are cursing and swear words. The Bible says that what comes out of a man's mouth is what's in his heart (Matthew 12:34, Luke 6:45). When we speak, we reveal the condition of our hearts...what and how we say things...sometimes it's more obvious than other times. "To profane" means "to treat with irreverence or disrespect; away from the temple." Each Christian is a temple of the Holy Spirit.

I Corinthians 3:16, "Don't you know that you yourselves are God's temple, and that God's spirit lives in you?" When we live lives that are profane, it means we are living lives that distance us from the one who is in the temple (our body), God. When Solomon dedicated the temple, the Glory of God (Shekinah) in a cloud came into it (1 Kings 8:10-11) and filled it. When we became Christians, the invisible glory of God came into us. God created all things, visible and invisible (Colossians 1:16). God created the part of us that is visible, our physical bodies, and the part of us that is invisible, our spirit. 1 Corinthians 6:19, "Do you not know that your body is a temple of the Holy Spirit, who is in you?" When we commit acts that grieve and quench... acts that profane the Holy Spirit...then we are creating that distance away from the temple, or, in this case, away from the one who inhabits the temple. What does God do? Where does he go when we commit acts of profaneness consistently and unrepentantly? God pulls back the fire of the Holy Spirit. He pulls back the Shekinah (the invisible Glory of God), and if taken far enough, Shekinah becomes Ichabod, which means "the glory has departed," or been put out.

1 Thessalonians 5:19, "Do not put out the Spirit's fire." We are distancing ourselves (profaning) from the glory of God by deliberate, unrepentant sin. It can come to the

point of Ichabod, ("the glory of God has departed") leaving no more proof that God is actively present. In other words, there is no evidence of God's light at work in our lives. God is not joined to adultery while his temple is being profaned. God is not joined to sexual immorality while his temple is being profaned. God is not joined to lust, murder, hate, greed, when we defile his temple by doing these things. It's bad enough that when Christians do bad things, God is considered "guilty by association" even though God is not literally involved, rather removed, or distanced from and by the sin itself.

James 4:4, "You adulterous people." Who is the writer talking to? He is descriptively referring to God's people. See how James 1:2 starts, "My brothers and sisters," then develops into James 4:4, "Anyone who chooses to be a friend of the world is an enemy of God." James 4: 4-6, "You adulterous people, don't you know that friendship with the world is hatred toward God? Anyone who chooses to be a friend of the world becomes an enemy of God. Or do you think that scripture says without reason that the spirit he caused to live in us envies intensely? But he gives us more grace."

Private Property Rights

The Holy Spirit lives in us and envies intensely. Why? Because the Christian temple belongs to him and whenever it is profaned, or violated, or vandalized, we're doing an injustice to something that belongs to him. God now owns us, and we are the caretakers of his temple. Remember, we are not our own. God lives in it, the temple (in us, that is), and he is experiencing our lives with us, in us, through us, and when we sin, we're refusing to let God continue to experience what is his because we're creating a distance from what is his, (us) when we defile the temple, our bodies, our lives.

Back to James 4:4-6, there were people in the group of brothers and sisters, fellow Christians, who were simultaneously called adulterers, at least spiritually speaking, because of their lifestyle choices, so much so that the writer of James was calling them out and holding them accountable. The idea here is that we can't serve two masters (Matthew 6:24).

God doesn't want competition, but if it happens, God still loves us and is more than willing to give us grace to overcome our sin. Scripture encourages us to come near to God. James 4:8 "Come near to God, and he will come near to you." If we have distanced ourselves from God by profane acts, we can also determine to turn our lives around and seek the grace from God that he offers. God will give us more grace to recover from the sins of the world, to recover from ourselves, and to find healing and reconciliation with him and others. When Solomon dedicated the temple (2 Chronicles 6:24-40), he prayed that if God's people were distanced from him, that if they came to their senses and prayed for recovery, God would hear and heal. It was and is called the ministry of reconciliation. That's the ministry that God is in; keeping what is his and recovering what was his. Remember, we have God's unconditional love, but we may not have God's unconditional approval. God adjoins himself directly to us, by being in us, and when we experience life, he experiences that life with us. When we go through things that are not directly sinful, he's experiencing it. He experiences our diseases, ailments, and treatments when we do. He experiences our emotions as we do. He lives in the Christian, and he feels that life as that person feels it. As earlier explained, even though God cannot adjoin our sin, he is experiencing the consequences of our sin with us. The epitome of God experiencing our sin was on the cross where he had to suffer the consequences of all sins. Yet, even in experiencing the consequences of our sin, God will never leave us or forsake us (Deuteronomy 31:8). We can be forgiven of our sins and still suffer the consequences of them. God will experience prison life with us, the loss of a marriage, the loss of a job, the loss of health, literally, because he's in us, he experiences our consequences, being the result of our sins, wrong choices, and destructive lifestyle choices. Hebrews 4:15, "For we do not have a high priest who is unable to empathize with our weaknesses, but we have one who has been tempted in every way, just as we are, yet was without sin."

He's Still There Doing That

We all have people in our lives who can't understand or empathize with what we're going through. They just don't get it. The husband who doesn't understand what it is to be a woman. Someone who never had kids lecturing someone who has successful kids. Someone giving marriage advice after having four divorces. The person giving investment advice after three bankruptcies. Some people are bad examples or have no successful experiences in what they are telling others, or they try to be a "Monday morning quarterback" for someone else's life. Some can't relate at all with what it's like to be in our shoes. We have someone who has been tempted (Hebrews 4:15) and because of that, he is able to deal gently with us. Christ has been there and done that, experienced life as a human like us, so he understands and he's still there doing that by experiencing the lives of his children. There is a difference between God's Omnipresence and God's Omni-experience. God's Omnipresence implies observer, God sees what's going on. God's Omni-experience implies being a participant, someone who's experientially involved at the core level. God is with us and in us at the same time; what we're going through, he's going through with us. Our concerns, fears, ambitions, trials, tribulations, longings, desires, hopes, dreams, losses, joy, peace, etc. He feels what we feel. He's in it with us.

God Experiences My Life

I have been crucified with Christ and I no longer live, but Christ lives in me. The life I now live in the body, I live by faith in the son of God who loved me and gave himself for me.
               Galatians 2:20

We are in it together. I have been crucified with Christ. Christ lives in me.

Ephesians 3:16-17, "I pray that out of his glorious riches, he may strengthen you with power through his Spirit in your inner being, so that Christ may dwell in your hearts through faith." Where? In our inner being, in our hearts. That is where the Spirit of God resides, dwells, and habituates in the holy of holies of the temple of our lives. God feels what we feel. What we're exposed to, he's exposed to. What's going through our minds and hearts, that is what God experiences on a second-by-second, minute-by-minute, hour-by-hour, and day-by-day basis. Week, month, and year after year, for each believer. 1 Corinthians 12:26, "If one part suffers, every part suffers with it. If one part is honored, every part rejoices with it." This is because of the intimate fellowship that we are to have with one another. How much more so with God? The emotions that we have are what he is exposed to and faced with directly. He experiences every range of emotion that we have. God is not greedy or selfish when we are, but those feelings and temptations are experienced by him through us. God is not lustful or abusive when we are, yet he experiences this as we do. God does not sin and is not a part of the actual, literal sin; he withdraws from that, but he experiences the desires and temptations of sin as we do, and he will give us the grace to overcome, avoid, or recover spiritually from our sin.

> *Do you not know that your bodies are members of Christ himself? Shall I then take the members of Christ and unite them with a prostitute? Never! Do you not know that he who unites himself with a prostitute is one with her in body? For it is said, "The two will become one flesh." But whoever is united with the Lord is united with him in spirit. Flee from sexual immorality. All other sins a person commits are outside the body, but whoever sins sexually, sins against their own body. Do you not know that your bodies are temples of the Holy Spirit, who is in you, whom you have received from God? You are not your own; you were bought at a price. Therefore, honor God with your bodies.*
> 1 Corinthians 6:15-20

A temple is a place dedicated to worship and having a divine presence or purpose. Our bodies are considered as temples, having the divine presence of God within us. The warning is to not defile the temple, it really isn't ours ("You are not your own..." Corinthians 3:23). When we defile the temple, we're in effect bringing shame and disrespect, or desecration to God's temple, and subsequently to God himself. We are not to "join" God's temple (our bodies) with sexual immorality. God is experiencing our lives as we are, and God refuses to be united with sin itself. When we partake in sin, we create the distancing from God by profaning our bodies.

Romans 12:1, "Therefore, I urge you, brothers and sisters, in view of God's mercy, to offer your bodies (temples) as living sacrifices, holy and pleasing to God— this is your spiritual act of worship." 1 Corinthians 3:16, "Don't you know that you yourselves are God's temple and that God's Spirit lives in you?" James 4:5, "Or do you think Scripture says without reason that the spirit he caused to live in us envies intensely?" God's word is quite clear on what to avoid and why; any other conclusion is to be in abject denial. God has a right to be angry, grieved, and to have a proper protecting jealousy when we misuse and abuse what belongs to him.

God has and continues to experience every demographic throughout the ages in the human drama, past and present. Galatians 3:28, "There is neither Jew nor Greek, slave nor free, male nor female, for you are all one in Christ Jesus." This is about the equality of Christ in us.

His Omni-Experience

Now consider this confession from the apostle Peter

in Acts 11:34-35, "Then Peter began to speak, 'I now realize how true it is that God does not show favoritism but accepts men from every nation who fear him and do what is right." God shows no favoritism, and God is not limited to experiencing what goes through different genders, nationalities, age groups, races, economic classes, the married, the single, the sick and the healthy, and any demographic imaginable. God is not limited to a man or a woman experience. He experiences our bodies the way we do. Because he experiences the Christian woman's life as she does, he is able to understand a woman's perspective on marriage, having children, and her place in the world. Because he is in his people no matter their ages, God understands a young woman's outlook and an old woman's mindset, for us and our children, young men, and old men. God understands the energy and vigor of youth and the restrictions and limitations of aging. He is in us, so he experiences our lives as they are lived.

God experiences different races and nationalities, the Asian in the crowded populations, the rural Mongolian in a hut, the tribal person in the jungles of South America or Africa. God knows what it's like to be a minority. God knows what it is to have a Jewish heritage, or an Italian, Irish, African, Hispanic, Asian or Arabic one. God experiences different economic classes. As he dwells in rich Christians, he knows both the trappings and advantages of wealth. God also experiences lives of poverty as he is in the lives of his people in the squalor of slums and tin shacks. God also can relate to middle-class suburbia and various occupations. God in his people across the spectrum of the labor force understands what is to be a doctor or nurse concerned over their patient, or an aide looking after the elderly in a care facility. He knows what it's like to be on the battlefield as a soldier, running into burning buildings as a firefighter, responding to distress calls as a law enforcement officer. He experiences life as a tradesman through his people while they are working on cars, building homes, making repairs, fixing machinery, picking up the garbage, ringing up the sales as a clerk, waiting on customers, selling cars, delivering goods, styling hair, coaching sports, and the list goes on. He experiences life as a business professional, requiring leadership and decision making to benefit the company and its product and employees.

God, while living in his people, experiences and understands what it is to lie in a hospital bed, suffering. He knows what it is to have the frustrations of teenage life and to grow a body. God understands every Christian's temptation and weakness. He knows what it's like to be tall or short, heavy, or thin. He experiences our disabilities or our physical fitness. He understands what it is to be intellectually disadvantaged. God lives the human life through each of his people, and that life as it was lived in its time. God isn't just experiencing our lives in the here and now but has also experienced each of his people's lives in the past. God experienced slavery as an African American. God experienced the Great Depression and those hard times. God experienced life in the colonial days of the United States of America. He also experienced life in the Middle Ages, as a slave, as a pauper.

God feels what we feel. Like the cancer treatments his children get. Like loneliness, or the betrayal of adultery. The anxiety of job loss. The struggle against addictions. The loss from divorce. He also experiences the joy of a baby's arrival, the excitement of a promotion. The feelings aren't his in origination, they are ours, but they are his experientially because he is in us. God experiences our failures, struggles, and successes. God is also in the recovery. God knows where we used to be, or where we never were. He's in our life with us through and through. It's true, we are not our own. Whatever our gender, age, class, stage of life, race, emotions, trials, that's also his life experience. He lives in each of his people, experiencing it with us.

> *You, dear children, are from God and have overcome them, because the one who is in you is greater than the one who is in the world.*
> 1 John 4:4

Summary

- I didn't say everything there is to say about the Omni-experience of God. I don't believe anyone could. As time goes on, more thoughts are thought, more things are said, and more dialogue has been had. Questions get asked and not all can be adequately answered.

- This is a revision of my original book, "Does God (Really) Understand What I'm Going Through." Originally written in 2015 and edited by Jen Meadows. All the experiential content in the original book, and this revision, are mine.

- God has experienced everything we have in principle or practice, as God, and/or as a human. He is experiencing everything that his people are experiencing, all at the same time, all the time, everywhere, as he lives in each of us. He is not just with you, he is in you, and you are not alone!

- God Is Experiencing Your Life!

Made in the USA
Middletown, DE
26 March 2023